VARDIS FISHER

Introductions to Mormon Thought

Edited by Matthew Bowman
and Joseph Spencer

*A list of books in the series appears
at the end of this book.*

VARDIS FISHER

A Mormon Novelist

MICHAEL AUSTIN

UNIVERSITY OF ILLINOIS PRESS
Urbana, Chicago, and Springfield

Library of Congress Cataloging-in-Publication Data
Names: Austin, Michael, 1966– author.
Title: Vardis Fisher: a Mormon novelist / Michael
    Austin.
Other titles: Introductions to Mormon thought
Description: Urbana: University of Illinois Press, [2021]
    | Series: Introductions to Mormon thought | Includes
    bibliographical references and index.
Identifiers: LCCN 2021019296 (print) | LCCN 2021019297
    (ebook) | ISBN 9780252044090 (cloth) | ISBN
    9780252086144 (paperback) | ISBN 9780252053030
    (ebook)
Subjects: LCSH: Fisher, Vardis, 1895–1968—Criticism and
    interpretation. | Mormon authors—20th century—
    Biography. | Western stories—History and criticism. |
    LCGFT: Biographies.
Classification: LCC PS3511.I744 Z55 2021 (print) | LCC
    PS3511.I744 (ebook) | DDC 813/.52 [B]—dc23
LC record available at https://lccn.loc.gov/2021019296
LC ebook record available at https://lccn.loc.gov/
    2021019297

For Gene England (1933–2001), who got here first.

Contents

Foreword to the Introductions
to Mormon Thought Series

Our purpose in this series is to provide readers with accessible and short introductions to important figures in the intellectual life of the religious movement that traces its origins to the prophetic career of Joseph Smith Jr. With an eye to the many branches of that movement (rather than solely to its largest branch, The Church of Jesus Christ of Latter-day Saints), the series gathers studies of what scholars have long called *Mormon* thought. We define "thought" and "intellectual life," however, quite as broadly as we define "Mormonism." We understand these terms to be inclusive, not simply of formal theological or scholarly work, but also of artistic production, devotional writing, institutional influence, political activism, and other non-scholarly pursuits. In short, volumes in the series assess the contributions of men and women who have shaped how those called Mormons in various traditions think about what "Mormonism" is.

We hope that this series marks something of a coming of age of scholarship on this religious tradition. For many years, Mormon studies have focused primarily on historical questions largely of internal interest to the (specifically) Latter-Day Saint community. Such historical work has also mainly addressed the nineteenth century. Scholars have accordingly established the key sources for the study of Mormon history and culture, and they have established a broad consensus on many issues surrounding the origins and character of the religious movement. Recent work, however, has pushed academics into the work of comparison, asking larger questions in two key ways. First, recent scholars have approached these topics from a greater variety of disciplines. There has emerged in Mormon studies, in other words, increasing visibility for the disciplines of philosophy, sociology, literary criticism, and media studies, among others. Second, scholars working this field have also begun to consider new topics of study—in particular gender and sexuality, the status of international Mormonism, and the experience of minority groups within the tradition. We believe the field has thus reached the point where the sort of syntheses these books offer is both possible and needed.

Michael Austin's study of Vardis Fisher is beautifully representative of the breadth of this series in both of its dimensions. Although Fisher drifted away from the Latter-day Saint faith by early adulthood, he retained a sense of identification with the religious tradition that Austin carefully analyzes. Fisher's literary works dealing with Mormonism revealed a deep intellectual engagement with the religion of his youth. Over time, Fisher has come to be recognized as a particularly important early representative of Mormonism in the literary world, and Austin ably examines the ways that Fisher's literary interactions with faith work at the often-blurry boundary between adherence to an American religious tradition and adherence to an American literary sensibility. Having quietly set the stage for what would become a long string of Mormon contributors to American letters, Fisher has waited long for the kind of attention he deserves from scholars working in Mormon studies—or from scholars of literature more generally. We are therefore pleased to include in *Introductions to Mormon Thought* Austin's careful examination of this important but too-often overlooked literary figure.

Matthew Bowman
Joseph Spencer

Acknowledgments

I could never have studied Fisher with the depth that he deserves without the help of many generous friends, so a few acknowledgments are in order

Ardis Parshall has transcribed and sent me hundreds of letters regarding Fisher and other writers that are stored in the archives of the Church of Jesus Christ of Latter-day Saints in Salt Lake City, and she also presented me with one of the few copies of *Dark Bridwell* left in the world. This is one of many projects that can be traced back to her talent and generosity.

My friend Bill Davis valiantly entered the special collections room at UCLA and came out with a large pile of letters between several LDS general authorities and the executives at 20th Century Fox in charge of the *Brigham Young* movie. Included in these letters was John A. Widstsoe's never-published review of *Children of God*, which I had been trying to find for several years, after seeing a number of allusions to it in his correspondence.

Another friend, Emily Gilliland Grover, agreed to assign one of her classes at Brigham Young University–Idaho the task of digitizing the collection of Vardis Fisher letters housed in their library. And June Can at the Beinecke Rare Book and Manuscript Library at Yale University graciously agreed to digitize and send me more than 700 pages of correspondence between Fisher and his agents and publishers. The special collections staff at Brigham Young University–Provo, the University of Utah, Weber State University, and Boise State University were all enormously helpful to me during the brief hours that I was able to spend working in their collections.

I am grateful to all of these friends and helpers, and I am grateful to *Dialogue: A Journal of Mormon Thought* for permission to reprint the material in Chapter Four that originally appeared in the Fall 2014 issue as "Vardis Fisher's Mormon Scars: Mapping the Diaspora in the *Testament of Man*."

But the most thanks go to my wife, Karen D. Austin, who insisted that either I get busy writing or get rid of the dozens of books by and about Fisher that I have accumulated over the years in the hopes of one day writing this book.

CHAPTER ONE

"Vardis Fisher Was Not a Mormon"

VARDIS FISHER WAS NOT A MORMON; did not have
a Mormon indoctrination during his formative years
in the home of his father [and] had apostatized from
the Mormon Church within a year after his baptism,
without ever having followed through on anything
that would have qualified him as a Mormon?

—Opal Laurel Holmes in an open letter to LDS
President Spencer W. Kimball

Religion is like smallpox. If you get a good dose,
you wear scars.

—Vardis Fisher, *We Are Betrayed*

Opal Laurel Holmes did not take kindly to people accusing her late husband
of Mormonism. One of the first people to find this out was the eminent
Mormon historian Leonard Arrington, who, together with John Haupt,
presented a paper entitled "The Mormon Heritage of Vardis Fisher" at the
inaugural conference of the Association for Mormon Letters in 1976. The
paper explored the possibility that Vardis Fisher's rejection of Mormonism
was less complete than critics had previously supposed. Against the common view of Fisher as an atheist who completely rejected Mormonism in
his youth, the authors argue that he "was not an apostate," that he "never
renounced his religion," and that "his outlook on life and history was religious, definitely Judeo-Christian and . . . definitely encompassing Latter-day
Saint belief and practice." The paper was published in *BYU Studies* the next
year, where it received modest exposure among scholars of Mormon and
Western American literature.[1]

Ms. Holmes was not amused. Between Fisher's death in 1968 and her
own death in 1994, she guarded her late husband's reputation with a jeal-

ousy that bordered on obsession. Convinced that Fisher would one day be remembered as a great American novelist, she felt a keen responsibility to make sure that nothing as nasty and disreputable as religion—especially Mormon religion—sullied his name. Holmes republished five of his out-of-print works under her own imprint, and to several of these she appended the statement "Vardis Fisher Was Not a Mormon." In her letter to Spencer W. Kimball, she demanded that he suitably reprimand anybody who claimed otherwise. Vardis Fisher may have once written a book about the Mormon migration, she insisted, but he was a freethinker, a seeker of truth, and a genuine intellectual—and definitely not a Mormon.

And yet, Fisher's association with Mormonism has always been one of the most identifiable things about him. He recognized this himself, and he identified himself as "of Mormon people" in publicity statements.[2] And these connections to Mormonism have become one of the main reasons that he continues to be relevant in the 21st century. As Mormonism begins to reach the status of a major world religion—with scholars, historians, and philosophers all trying to understand its development and its place in the world—a writer like Vardis Fisher becomes an important object of study. Literary critics need literature to criticize, and historians need people who did interesting things. Fisher lived a fascinating life and wrote 26 mainly well-received novels—about a third of which had at least something to do with Mormonism.

After his 20th birthday, Fisher never claimed Mormon beliefs as his beliefs. But he consistently claimed the Mormon tradition as his tradition and the Mormon people as his people. And these things matter to the way that we identify him today. "I don't believe any other person is more familiar with the essential facts of Mormon history and especially with the *spirit* of it than I am," he once wrote in a letter to his agent as she prepared to pitch *Children of God* to the major New York publishing houses. "My people on both sides were Mormons almost from the beginning. I was reared in the tradition and have in my blood and training the *spiritual feel* of the Church and its background."[3]

The facts of Fisher's life support his understanding of himself as the product of a Mormon upbringing. Fisher was born into a Mormon family and absorbed some elements of Mormon history and doctrine from his parents—along with a strong sense of his own Mormon identity. He was educated in Mormon ward schools until he was sixteen, and he attended a Mormon ward in Rigby while he was there for high school. He was officially baptized at the age of 20 and he likely considered serving a mission.[4] Within a year of his baptism, though, he left the Church and never returned. Yet he continued to write about Mormonism and identify himself as a product of the frontier religion that nearly all of the members of his family still accepted as the word of God. And, as Fisher spent most of his life illustrating in his autobiographical and genealogical novels, he did not believe that anybody, least of all himself, could completely escape the confines of the traditions in which they are raised.

The Early Years

Vardis Alvero Fisher was born in 1895 in Annis, Idaho, an unincorporated section of Jefferson County about five miles north of Rigby. The oldest child of parents descended from Mormon pioneers, he was named after his great-grandfather, Vardis John Fisher, who joined the Church of Jesus Christ of Latter-day Saints in 1834 and accompanied Joseph Smith in both Kirtland and Nauvoo. All four of his grandparents crossed the plains in the mid-19th century—though his mother's parents took a detour through Beaver Island, Michigan, as followers of James Strang, one of several claimants to Joseph Smith's prophetic mantle.[5]

Vardis's parents—Joseph and Temperance Fisher—met and married in the sparsely populated Mormon colony of Annis, where their families had been sent by Brigham Young to colonize the Snake River Valley.[6] By the time that Joseph and Temperance were married, though, all of the land near Annis had been claimed. So Joseph moved his young family—including five-year-old Vardis, his younger brother Vivian, and their infant sister Irene—to an isolated shack and four acres of river bottom that the previous owner traded to Joseph for a cow. The only other people within ten miles of them lived across the river. Without a bridge or a boat, they could visit only when it was warm enough to swim.[7]

Fisher later described in painful detail, his experience as a six-year-old boy leaving his home in Annis, driving all day in a horse-drawn wagon, and arriving at a "crumbling, cottonwood-log shack, with an earth roof and an earth floor and door hinges made out of old shoes."[8] This would be his family's home for ten years, where Joe and Patience Fisher shaped his views about morality, work, sexuality, and religion. It is also where he became a reader, despite the fact that the only books in his house were "a Bible, a Book of Mormon, and a few tattered copies of cheap novels."[9] Fisher was primarily attracted to the Bible. "I was an abnormally terrified, serious, and studious child," he wrote in 1953. "I learned to read at a very early age, and read everything that our impoverished home afforded, including the Bible. I read that book at least two or three times before I reached adolescence."[10]

Despite their poverty, the Fishers valued education for their children—especially since, for second-generation Mormon pioneers, they had such a small family. When Vardis was eleven years old, his mother sent him and his brother to live with an aunt and attend the LDS ward school thirty miles away in Annis.[11] A year later they transferred to another ward school in Poplar—only 15 miles from the Fisher homestead—where they lived by themselves in a vacant house that their mother provisioned with food and other necessities.[12] When the Fisher boys graduated from the ward school, they moved to Rigby to attend the region's only high school, which opened in 1912. While there, Vardis began attending the local Church of Jesus Christ of Latter-day Saints, and, on April 4, 1915, he was baptized along with his brother. In a semiautobiographical novel published in 1932, Fisher has his alter ego, Vridar Hunter, decline a Mormon mission call just a few weeks after his baptism, when a high school teacher convinces him that there is no such thing as sin. In a 1960 revision of the same novel, Vridar's decision not to serve a mission became a dramatic and permanent renunciation of Mormonism. "He knew that he was Mormon no more," concludes the first section of *Orphans in Gethsemane*. When school was ended and he had his diploma he did not wait for a parent to come with the wagon, but set out to walk."[13]

The existing records suggest that his departure from the Church may have been more gradual. Shortly after his baptism, the entire Fisher family traveled to Utah to be sealed in the Salt Lake Temple.[14] And that fall, he enrolled as a freshman at the University of Utah. His letters home assure his parents that he is continuing to live by Church standards, even as he complains that he is too busy studying to go to church.[15] While at the university, he continued to pursue Leona McMurtrey, the Mormon woman that he had fallen in love with back in Idaho. Vardis and Leona were married by a Mormon bishop on September 10, 1917. Soon after they were married, America entered World War I, and Vardis joined the Air Force with the idea of becoming a pilot. Leona moved back in with her parents in

Antelope, where their first son, Grant Fisher, was born in October of 1918. Vardis soon became disillusioned with the Air Force, and, after only a few months, he resigned from the service and returned to Idaho. But instead of returning to Antelope to be with his wife and newborn son, he went to Idaho Falls, where he helped his father start an auto mechanic business. Soon thereafter, his brother was drafted into the Army, and Vardis decided to accompany him. He joined the military for the second time in a year and went to San Diego with Vivian. As they were preparing to be shipped overseas, however, the war ended, and they were both sent home to Idaho Falls where Vardis was able to earn enough money to return to Salt Lake City to finish his bachelor's degree.[16]

While at the University of Utah, Fisher participated actively in both the Department of English and in the student literary magazine, *The University Pen*. He published his first work of fiction in December of 1916—a three-page story titled "Whose Mother?" consisting of a single conversation between a desperately poor older woman and an equally poor young boy who meet by chance and discuss the true meaning of Christmas. Between 1916 and 1923, Fisher published two more short stories, a handful of poems, and a one-act play in *The University Pen*, making it the first publication to nurture his growing literary ambitions. Fisher also wrote four other plays that he passed around the department and showed to his professors, earning him a reputation as a talented and intellectually serious student.[17]

Fisher impressed the literature faculty at the University of Utah enough that they offered him a teaching position after he graduated—with the condition that he pursue graduate studies and work toward a PhD In 1920 and 1921, Fisher split his time between Salt Lake City, where he taught Freshman Composition and Literature courses at the University of Utah, and Chicago, where he studied for his master's degree in literature at the University of Chicago. For most of this time, he and Leona lived apart and saw each other only when he came back to Utah or Idaho. But in September of 1921, Leona moved to Chicago, five months pregnant with their second child, and the Fishers settled in for the long haul of completing his master's degree and studying for his PhD.[18]

In Chicago, Vardis and Leona began to live together for the first time in their marriage. Things did not go well. The problems that had plagued their marriage from the start—Vardis's intense devotion to his schoolwork, Leona's feelings of isolation, and the growing religious and educational

6

gaps between them—became much worse when they were separated from their families and their home culture. For several years, Vardis's letters home expressed his dissatisfaction with Leona and, specifically, with her desire to have more children in order to fulfill what she perceived to be her religious duty. On Christmas Eve of 1921, Fisher wrote a lengthy letter to "Everybody" back in Idaho. He explained his disgust with the Mormon belief that parents should have many children to give bodies to spirits waiting in the pre-existence to be born. "You think there are millions of dear babes waiting to be born," he wrote. "I think that is all tommyrot. But granting that such is the case, I believe that it were better a thousand times for them never to be born than to be born as most people are today." And he tells his family that their attitude is "the most selfish and most unchristian thing I ever heard of" and that "under the guise of religion such people as you unconsciously bring about more suffering than a world of reformatory societies could take care of."

In this letter, Fisher makes it very clear that his break with Mormonism is complete, and that 99 percent of Christians, including Mormons, are despicable, damnable, sneaking, cowardly hypocrites. He declares himself free of religious constraints and proclaims that he now has a religion of his own with his own ten commandments (always the overachiever, he actually gives twenty—ten things he rejects and ten things he accepts). He rejects, for example, baptism, prayer, churches, evangelism, a personal God, and "cutting down a million young pines every year for Christmas trees. He accepts tolerance, freedom of thought, authenticity, and universal love. And, significantly, the new religion he creates for himself is built from the ashes of his Mormon upbringing. "I do believe in the last article of the Principles of Faith of the Mormon Church," he declares as his first positive belief, "and I make it the basis of my religion." Fisher refers here to the Thirteenth Article of Faith of the Church of Jesus Christ of Latter-day Saints, which reads, "We believe in being honest, true, chaste, benevolent, virtuous, and in doing good to all men; indeed, we may say that we follow the admonition of Paul—We believe all things, we hope all things, we have endured many things, and hope to be able to endure all things. If there is anything virtuous, lovely, or of good report or praiseworthy, we seek after these things."[19]

In 1924, Fisher reported to his parents, and to Leona, that he had fallen in love with a fellow graduate student named Margaret Trusler. He felt that she was his intellectual and creative equal and that he would be unable to realize his greatest ambition—to be a writer of important books—if he were shackled with an unsympathetic wife and needy children. In a long letter to his mother, he wrote that "the driving force of my life is the desire to write" and that "if I stay with my family, I must give up my ambitions and . . . die." The only wife he could incorporate into his life's plan was a woman "who understands me and what I want to do, who wants to do the same thing, who burns as I burn to render a great service to the human race, who is unselfish, loyal, unafraid."[20] Margaret Trusler, he felt, was such a woman, and his wife Leona was not.

On September 8, 2024, Leona McMurtrey Fisher committed suicide by drinking household disinfectant while she and Vardis were arguing. Fisher, not without reason, blamed himself, and he never got over the guilt. "Fisher's life was almost completely ruined by the grief caused by his wife Leona's suicide," wrote Joseph M. Flora in his 1965 book-length study of Fisher's work. "As he makes abundantly clear, it was his own failure to make sense of his life that had lead Leona to this step."[21] In order to understand his own failure and try to make sense of his experiences, he devoted the next ten years of his life to telling the story of their courtship and marriage in the four autobiographical novels that he would refer to as his "tetralogy."

Becoming a Writer

Within a year of Leona's death, Vardis completed his dissertation on the English novelist and poet Gorge Meredith, graduated magna cum laude from the University of Chicago with a PhD in English Literature, and returned to Salt Lake City to accept the position he had been promised on the English faculty. A year later, Margaret Trusler found a job in the same department and joined him in Utah. Fisher was now a professor, but all he really wanted to be was a writer. He had neither the time nor the inclination to do the work necessary to succeed as a member of a college faculty. He didn't like teaching classes and had no interest in departmental or university politics. And he was openly contemptuous of the Mormon religion, to which most of the students and faculty of the University of Utah belonged—and which exercised considerable influence with the officially secular administration.[22]

Fisher spent most of his time in Salt Lake City writing novels and submitting them to publishers. But he also wrote poetry, which would lead

8

to his first published book, albeit a self-published one. In the months that followed Leona's death, Vardis wrote poems to her memory that blended the sentimental child he had once been and the rational humanist he was quickly becoming. He found a ready audience for his poetry in the little magazines run by the New York poet and editor Harold Vinal, and he published several of these poems in Vinal's *Voices: An Open Forum for the Poets*.[23] Vinal also operated a subsidy publishing imprint, and, in 1927, Fisher paid him $400 to publish a book of 72 poems under the title, *Sonnets to an Imaginary Madonna*. "It was a 'vanity' project and I should have been kicked and put to bed," Fisher admitted some twelve years later. "The *Sonnets* have a few good lines . . . but on the whole they're the sort of thing an author wants to forget."[24] But Fisher continued to write and publish poetry well into the 1930s, publishing his poems in Eastern magazines and Western regional anthologies—and sprinkling them liberally throughout his semiautobiographical tetralogy.[25]

Fisher really wanted to write novels, though, and during the time he spent in Utah, he wrote six manuscripts and submitted them to agents and publishers. The first five were rejected by every publisher he approached.[26] The sixth, however, found gold when *Toilers of the Hills*—a novel based on the life of Fisher's uncle, who was among the first to apply dryland farming techniques in Southern Idaho—was accepted by the prestigious Houghton Mifflin Co. of Boston. *Toilers of the Hills* was published in 1928 to largely positive reviews. On the strength of these reviews, and his PhD from the University of Chicago, Fisher was offered a teaching position at Washington Square College of New York University. In the Fall of 1928, Fisher resigned his position at the University of Utah and moved to Manhattan, where he and Margaret were married.

Founded in 1914 as NYU's undergraduate commuter campus, Washington Square College had an open admission policy and soon became a popular alternative to the main campus, whose admission standards at the time placed restrictive quotas on the number of Jewish and Catholic students offered admission.[27] The new college grew explosively in the 1920s. The college pursued up-and-coming writers—who were eager to live in New York City where nearly all the agents and publishing houses were located—to teach Freshman English at a very modest salary. When Fisher arrived on campus, he found himself surrounded by other young and aspiring writers who had been declared "promising" by the senior faculty members. One of these young writers—a tall young man from North Carolina named Thomas Wolfe—had just signed a contract with Scribner's to publish *Look Homeward, Angel*.

Fisher and Wolfe quickly became friends, united by their shared interest in a particular type of fiction. *Look Homeward, Angel* is a highly confessional novel based on the author's own life and set in a region largely unknown to most Eastern readers. Fisher had already completed a similar novel called *In Tragic Life*, based on his own childhood in rural Idaho. On Wolfe's suggestion, Fisher submitted the manuscript to Max Perkins at Scribner's, who had accepted and then substantially revised *Look Homeward, Angel*. But Perkins rejected Fisher's, as did nearly every other New York publisher of note—often on the grounds that, while powerful and well written, its profanity and graphic sexuality would alienate readers and run afoul of the antiobscenity laws that prevented James Joyce's *Ulysses* from being published in the United States until 1933.[28] Fisher's own publisher, Houghton Mifflin, rejected *In Tragic Life* with a note that it was "too strong meat for our table."[29]

Fisher did place a second novel with Houghton Mifflin, though: *Dark Bridwell*, a story set in the same world as both *Toilers of the Hills* and *In Tragic Life*. Like *Toilers*, *Dark Bridewell* was almost universally praised by Eastern literary critics as a direct and powerful example of regionalism in modern fiction. And like his first novel, *Dark Bridwell* was almost universally ignored by the reading public. His publication agreement with Houghton Mifflin stipulated that he would not receive any royalties until the book sold 2,000 copies (*Toilers of the Hills* had sold 3,000). *Dark Bridwell* sold only 800 copies, and Fisher never received any money from it until 1952, when it was published in paperback with a lurid cover and the title *The Wild Ones*.[30] Meanwhile, *Look Homeward, Angel* became a literary phenomenon and launched Wolfe into the top rank of American novelists. For the rest of his career, Fisher was accused of imitating his friend Thomas Wolfe with his own series of confessional novels, even though, as he pointed out on multiple occasions, he had completed *In Tragic Life* before he ever met Thomas Wolfe or heard about *Look Homeward, Angel*.[31]

By 1931, it had become clear to Fisher that teaching Freshman English in New York was doing nothing to advance his writing career. "I had to make a choice between teaching and writing books," he later recalled.[32] So, at the end of the 1931 spring term, he and Margaret left New York and returned to

Idaho, where he would spend the rest of his life—with the exception of two summer terms and one fall semester as a visiting professor at the University of Montana in 1931 and 1932. Vardis Fisher chose a precarious time to leave a secure job in New York and move back to Idaho. By the summer of 1931, the Great Depression had plunged the nation into chaos—and the states that depended on agriculture were hit especially hard. But Fisher believed that he could be a great writer, and he intuitively understood that the best way for him to do so was to return to his native soil.

When he returned to Idaho, he decided to stop trying to sell New York publishers on *In Tragic Life*. Instead, he submitted it to the Caxton Printers of Caldwell, Idaho—a printing company that had begun publishing regional fiction only a few years earlier. Caxton would become an important part of Fisher's career, and its owner, James Herrick (J. H.) Gipson, would become one of his best friends over the next 20 years. In 1932 Fisher approached Gipson after being rejected by nearly every major publisher on the East Coast. Fisher later recalled what happened next: "He sent the manuscript to an eminent Western editor. The editor said that it was a 'powerful and beautiful' story that ought to be published, but it was no book for Gipson to undertake. 'If you print it,' he wrote, 'Idaho will probably drive you from its borders; because the response to this novel, both in your State and over the nation, will be an angry storm of protest.'" When Gipson got this review, according to a promotional pamphlet published by Caxton in 1939, Gipson announced, "I'll publish the book if I have to walk barefoot down the streets."[33]

Caxton published *In Tragic Life in 1932* to largely positive reviews, and several of the Eastern firms who had initially rejected it approached Fisher with second thoughts. Doubleday, Doran & Co. brought Gipson out to New York to negotiate a shared publication agreement, and the book was reissued the following year jointly by Caxton and Doubleday—as were the three sequels *Passions Spin the Plot* (1934), *We Are Betrayed* (1935), and *No Villain Need Be* (1936).

Despite everything the book had going for it—joint publication with a large national press, enthusiastic reviews in newspapers across the country, a cover painting by Grant Wood that became a minor masterpiece, and the good fortune to become an alternate selection of the Book-of-the-Month Club—*In Tragic Life* sold fewer than 2000 copies, and the subsequent volumes sold even fewer.

But the critical praise heaped on Fisher by the Eastern literary establishment helped to transform Caxton into the most prominent book publisher in the American West. Almost overnight, the small-town printer 2500 miles away from New York City—whose five-year-old trade-book division had mainly published works by Gipson's family members—found itself in a partnership with the largest publishing company in the country.[34] Gipson used this attention to promote regional literature from the West, and specifically from Idaho, to national and international audiences. This allowed Caxton to launch the careers of many Western writers of both fiction and nonfiction—including George Dixon Snell, Richard Summers, Marguerite Cameron, Reva Stanley. Lawrence Henry Gipson, James's brother, who published his first three books with Caxton, went on to win both the Bancroft Prize and the Pulitzer Prize for history.[35]

The Great Depression

By 1935 Vardis Fisher was widely considered a rising literary star. His books had been published with two of the most respected publishing houses in the country—Houghton Mifflin and Doubleday, Doran—and reviewed favorably in the *New York Times*, the *Chicago Tribune*, the *Saturday Review*, the *London Times*, and dozens of smaller newspapers and magazines throughout the world. Both he and his wife had PhDs from one of the most prestigious universities in the country. And they were completely broke, living in a one-room cabin behind his parents' house in Idaho with no prospect of being able to maintain even that spartan lifestyle in the middle of the Great Depression.

Though Vardis Fisher did not support Roosevelt's New Deal, the New Deal was destined to support Vardis Fisher. In the fall of 1935 he received a brief telegram from Washington, D.C., offering him the position of Idaho State Director for the Federal Writers' Project—a department of the Works Progress Administration (WPA) that employed out-of-work writers to create materials deemed important to the public interest. At its height, the Federal Writers' Project employed more than 6,600 people across the country, including such future luminaries as Saul Bellow, Nelson Algren, Richard Wright, Zora Neal Hurston, Juanita Brooks, John Steinbeck, Ralph Ellison, and John Cheever.[36] The initial goal of the project was to produce a series of comprehensive state guides that included information about the history, geography, populations, folklore, and culture of each American state. As a state director, Fisher would be responsible for hiring talented writers from Idaho and coordinating their efforts to produce a guide.

Fisher did not want the job. Like most Westerners of his day, he distrusted the federal government and resented its attempts to manage the nation's interior from the East Coast. And he despised both Roosevelt and the New Deal. But the salary of $2,200 a year was more than he had ever made, and he had no other viable sources of income.[37] "It looks now as if I shall accept supervision of PWA writers' project in Idaho," he wrote to his agent, Elizabeth Nowell. "I feel absurd in going into this work but when a man is financially against a wall and has two sons soon ready for college he does absurd things."[38]

Fisher immediately faced serious difficulties in recruiting competent writers from Idaho's unemployed population.[39] But he was willing to do all of the work himself, and as a result, the Idaho office soon became the star of the Federal Writers' Program—and not always in a good way. His superiors in Washington praised the quality of his work. But when Fisher announced that the Idaho guide was ready for publication, and that he had already arranged with Caxton Press to publish it, the supervisors panicked. Henry Alsberg, the director of the Federal Writers' Project, had always intended for the Washington, D.C., Guide to be the first volume published. Not only did he consider it appropriate to unveil a national writing project in the nation's capital; he also needed to make the initial offering visible to members of Congress, who had deep reservations about putting thousands of writers on the public payroll. A Washington guide would be noticed by Congress immediately; an Idaho guide would hardly be noticed at all.

Alsberg sent multiple telegrams to Fisher demanding last-minute format changes or copyedits, trying to slow him down long enough for the Washington, D.C., team to finish their volume. But Fisher ignored the orders and, after a while, "consign[ed] them to the furnace without bothering to read them."[40] For Fisher, publishing the first volume in the series was a matter of pride, and poking the useless Washington, D.C., bureaucrats in the eye was an additional benefit. In January of 1937, Caxton Press published the 431-page *Idaho: A Guide in Words and Pictures*, the first volume of the Federal Writers' Project American Guides Series. And though Fisher had angered nearly everybody else associated with the project, the reviews of the volume were overwhelmingly positive.[41] "If all the state books which follow measure up to the standard set by the Idaho book," wrote the enthusiastic reviewer from the *Boston Post*, "then critics all over the nation will acclaim the federal writers' project."[42]

As the glowing reviews poured in, it became clear to Alsberg that Fisher had brought credit to the project. His insubordination, which could well have cost Fisher the best job he had ever had, was forgiven if not entirely forgotten.[43] Fisher went on to publish two more substantial volumes as the project director: *The Idaho Encyclopedia* (1938) and *Idaho Lore* (1939), along with a fourth—a guide to Boise—that was not published until Laura Johnston and Alessandro Meregaglia rediscovered and published it in 2019.[44] During the same period, Fisher published two of his own novels—*April* (1937) and *Forgive Us Our Virtues* (1938)—both based on material he had been working on for years. *April*, which Fisher considered the best of all his books, was a comic novel set in Antelope Hills and published by Doubleday, Doran. *Forgive Us Our Virtues*, the first Fisher novel published by Caxton without a New York partner, was a psychological novel about a group of interconnected people slowly discovering the deceptions they practiced on each other and on themselves. Critics praised *April* and panned *Forgive Us Our Virtues*, but neither book sold more than a few hundred copies, and Doubleday, Doran finally dropped Fisher as an author.[45]

By 1938, however, Fisher had a new novel ready to shop around—one that he had been working on for the entire time that he had been directing the Idaho Writers' Project and that he considered "the crucial novel of my career."[46] In his various query letters in 1938, he referred to it simply as "the Mormon novel." It would go on to be published under the title *Children of God*—and it would become the biggest success of his career. By the beginning of 1939, several major New York publishers were competing for the right to publish it, but the strongest contender was Harper & Brothers, who sponsored the biannual Harper Novel Prize—by far the richest literary prize in the United States at the time. Fisher eventually signed with Harper, and, on June 26, 1939, *Children of God* was awarded the Harper Prize, with a guaranteed advance of $7,500 (about $140,000 in 2020 dollars), or close to three years' salary for the Director of the Idaho Writers' Project. He earned another $4,400 when Hollywood producer Darryl Zanuck purchased the film rights for a movie about Brigham Young that was already in production.[47]

The success of *Children of God* meant that Fisher no longer had to work for the federal government he despised. He used his prize money to build a house in Hagerman, a rural area about a hundred miles southeast of Boise, and he resigned from his position with the Federal Writers' Project.[48] The end of his time in Boise corresponded to the end of his marriage to Margaret. Their marriage had been difficult for years, and since the birth of their first child together—Fisher's third son—their differences had become irreconcilable. For several years, Fisher had been having an affair with Opal Holmes, his research assistant, who was nearly 20 years his junior. In 1939, Vardis and Margaret divorced, and in 1940 he married Holmes, and they moved to their new house in Hagerman.[49]

At this point, Vardis Fisher was 45 years old, and the trajectory of his life had hardened into a routine that he would maintain for the rest of his life. From 1940 until his death in 1968, he and Opal lived in the same house, where he kept up his daily routine of writing every morning and doing heavy farm labor every afternoon.[50] He supplemented his income by writing editorial columns for Idaho newspapers espousing his trademark blend of atheism, libertarian conservatism, and militant anticommunism. From 1940 until about 1956, these three activities each provided roughly a third of his income, which rarely rose above $4,000 a year, even when dividends from earlier investments were added into the mix. Many years it was closer to $3,000.[51]

Fisher could have done much better financially if he had spent the rest of his career writing Western-themed novels for popular audiences. After the success of *Children of God*, his editor at Harper told him that he could guarantee $10,000 a year if he would stick to the Western historical formula and produce a novel every two years.[52] And he did write one follow-up novel for Harper called *City of Illusion*, which dealt with the discovery of silver in Nevada and the subsequent Silver Rush of 1859. But Fisher had no intention of spending the rest of his life in a box marked "Western Americana," no matter how lucrative. He had much grander plans for his life.

For several years, Fisher had been planning to write a series of novels tracing the evolution of human civilization, with an emphasis on the way that humans became ashamed of their sexual instincts and turned to religious myths to try to suppress them—an impulse that played a large part in his own autobiographical writings. For the next 20 years, Fisher would devote almost all his time and energy to this project. And though he wrote prolifically over those years—producing 16 novels, 2 nonfiction books, and 1 collection of short fiction—he would never again experience either the critical or the commercial success that came with *Children of God*.[53]

The *Testament of Man*

Fisher first began discussing his idea for a series of historical novels with his agent, Elizabeth Nowell, in 1938. During negotiations for *Children of God*, Fisher brought up the idea of pitching "the series" to Harper editor Ed Aswell as part of a package deal.[54] But even though Harper accepted both *Children of God* and *City of Illusion*, they had no interest in publishing the series. "I've known for a long while that [Aswell] has no enthusiasm for it," he wrote Nowell in November of 1940. "And I am well aware that I perhaps could make from ten thousand a year up if I were content to be a historical novelist and write for money. But that has never been my intention. I've been holing in here and getting ready to live again, if necessary, on a few hundred a year."[55]

Fisher parted ways with Harper in 1941, and he developed an intriguing strategy to kickstart the series that, he realized, would not be attractive to most Eastern publishers. He wrote a third Western historical novel, *The Mothers*, which told the story of the Donner Party's ill-fated expedition through the Sierra Nevada Mountains in 1846 and 1847. He offered this to publishers as part of a two-book deal along with the as-yet untitled first novel of his series—a strange piece of psychological fiction from the perspective of an early human ancestor (*Australopithecus anamensis*) who roamed the African savannah two million years ago.

The ploy worked, and he sold both books to Vanguard Press—a small, but respectable New York publishing house that helped to launch the careers of, among others, Saul Bellow, Nelson Algren, Joyce Carol Oates, and Dr. Seuss.[56] In 1942, Vanguard published both *The Mothers* and Fisher's new novel, which they titled *Darkness and the Deep*. Vanguard agreed to at least consider subsequent volumes in the series, and Fisher, convinced that he had a publisher for the long haul, settled in to write what he saw as the novels that would define him as a writer and artist. He called the series "The *Testament of Man*," and his initial letter to Vanguard set out the plan for a series of "about eight novels" whose purpose would be "to throw some sort of searchlight down the past and discover some reasons, if they are discoverable (and I think they are) why the human race has evolved into the mess it seems to be in today." To do this, Fisher proposed to research deeply into established academic disciplines and "try to give in continuity the development of our chief attitudes, superstitions, cults, and moral

"Vardis Fisher Was Not a Mormon"

values. The race is carrying a hell of a lot of dead and useless burdens today and only students in these fields seem to know it."[57]

The *Testament of Man* ultimately ran to twelve full-length novels, for which Fisher reported reading more than 2,000 works of contemporary scholarship in archeology, anthropology, ethnology, history, religious studies, and philosophy.[58] It begins with *Australopithecus anamensis* and ends with a rewritten version of the tetralogy titled *Orphans in Gethsemane*, with Vridar Hunter as the logical endpoint of a series of forked paths that his ancestors took: the Cro-Magnons exterminated the Neanderthals (Book 2), matriarchal society became patriarchal (Books 3 and 4), the people chose prophets over kings (Books 5 and 6), the Hellenistic Jews were defeated by the fundamentalist Maccabees (Book 7), the Christian Church gradually embraced asceticism and self-renunciation instead of abundance (Books 8–10) and became a corrupt and oppressive regime (Book 11). Each of the novels features at least one creative, introspective genius who mirrors the Vridar Hunter of the tetralogy. The choices that these characters make, and the ways that their societies respond to their choices, lead inexorably to the neurotic, guilt-ridden, frustrated fictional truth seeker named Vridar Hunter—and to his real-life alter ego Vardis Fisher.

The *Testament of Man* series was plagued by two problems from the very beginning. First, the books did not sell well. None of them sold more than a few thousand copies, and sales declined as the series progressed. Second, the series offended the religious sensibilities of almost everyone who read them, especially Jews and Christians, whose origins and doctrines were presented unfavorably in many of the volumes. Vanguard dropped the series after the fifth book, *The Divine Passion*, unwilling to risk the backlash for publishing the sixth volume, *The Valley of Vision*, which presented Solomon as a worldly monarch who tried unsuccessfully to curb the influence of the Yahweh cult in Israel.

An even smaller company called Abelard Press picked up the series and published *Valley of Vision* and its sequel, *The Island of the Innocent*—a love story set in the midst of the Maccabean rebellion. The main editor at Abelard, Fred Marsh, had been one of Fisher's earliest boosters and had written the front-page review of *Children of God* for the *New York Times*. After Marsh left, however, Abelard balked at publishing the eighth novel in the series, which Fisher had titled *Sing, Ye Heavens*. This novel presented Jesus Christ as a non-divine Jewish peasant named Joshua who allows himself to be seen as the Messiah when he realizes that the Jews need someone to believe in. In October of 1952, Fisher received a curt letter from Abelard stating that "it would not be advantageous to attempt to market the book."[59] This was the fifth time in his career that Fisher had been dropped by an Eastern publishing house, and it was very unlikely that another would pick him up. No mainstream publishing company in 1953 wanted to publish a book denying the divinity of Jesus Christ. The public backlash would have been furious and immediate. And even if a brave editor might have been willing to take such a risk for the right novel, they would not take it for the eighth book in a series whose most recent installments had sold only a few hundred copies each.

From the moment that he started the series, though, Fisher knew that Gipson would publish any of the volumes that could not be placed else-where—and he frequently used this knowledge as a negotiation point with his publishers. When Vanguard asked him to change some sexually explicit material in one of the books, he pushed back, "Gipson will always print my stuff as I write it, and censors be damned."[60] And when he pitched the Jesus book to Lippincott, he wrote "Caxton Printers are ready to see me to the end of my literary life" so "it is solely a question whether I am to find a larger house."[61] When he despaired of finding anyone to publish the rest of the series, Fisher wrote to his agent that "If worst comes to worst I'll go back to Caxton."[62] Caxton had been involved in the project from the beginning, with Gipson issuing deluxe, leather-bound editions of the first seven books.

So, when Fisher sent the manuscript to Caxton in 1953, Gipson shocked him by refusing to publish it unless it was approved by a Catholic theologian. Though he was an avowed atheist like Fisher, Gipson was even more violently anticommunist, and he saw Christianity as the last bulwark against communist aggression. Fisher was incensed. He shot back a letter to Gipson complaining that he was being asked "to submit this novel to a fanatic and an apologist for the Roman Church" and charging that "the judgment would be worthless." He closed the letter by expressing his grief at being treated this way by a friend: "That I am deeply distressed to find you taking such a position after our long and close relationship goes without saying. That I shall in any respect withdraw from the findings of the greatest scholars is unthinkable, even if the novels are never published."[63] He and Gipson never spoke again.

Without Caxton to serve as a backstop as it had done since 1935, Fisher had nowhere to go. He became despondent and stopped writing altogether for a time. And then he went back to his former strategy of trying to use Western historical novels to lure publishers into a relationship with him and accept the remaining five volumes of the *Testament of Man* as well. For several years he had been contemplating a novel about the skirmishes between rival trading companies in the Hudson Bay Colony in the early part of the 19th century. He began to write this book and instructed his agent to try to place it and the Jesus Book at the same firm.[64] Fisher eventually sold the novel to Doubleday and published it with the title *Pemmican* in 1957. The book sold well enough that Doubleday bought a follow-up novel, *Tale of Valor*, about the Lewis and Clark expedition. But they wanted only the Western books. Neither they nor any other publisher that Fisher approached had any interest in the Jesus novel or any of the other remaining volumes in the *Testament of Man*.

One publisher was interested in the series, however. Alan Swallow was a highly respected English professor and director of the University of Denver Press when he left the university in 1954 to focus on his own publishing firm, Alan Swallow Books.[65] Like J. H. Gipson in 1926, Swallow—who came from rural Montana—wanted to publish the literature of the American West, and he considered Vardis Fisher one of its most important figures.[66] Swallow had heard through his friends in the publishing world that Fisher's *Testament of Man* series had stalled and that even Caxton had abandoned it. He wrote Fisher in 1954 asking him about the status of the series and expressing an interest in publishing it. Fisher still hoped to get an Eastern publisher, but, after disappointing near misses at Scribner's and Harcourt Brace, he decided to accept Swallow's offer and restart the series.

After a four-year hiatus, the eighth volume of the *Testament of Man* finally appeared in 1956 as *Jesus Came Again*—a title designed to place some distance between Fisher's Joshua and the biblical Jesus. Fisher and Swallow prepared (and likely hoped) for the inevitable backlash by outraged Christians. But the backlash never came. *Jesus Came Again*—the book that had cost Fisher four years of his life and one of his most important friendships—received just a handful of reviews and had virtually no sales. Nobody protested its portrayal of Jesus Christ because nobody bothered to read it, and Swallow estimated that he lost $3,000 on its publication.[67] That same year, Swallow also published the ninth installment of the *Testa-*

ment of Man series—a heavily annotated novel about Roman Christianity called *A Goat for Azazel*.

Vardis Fisher was back, and he sprinted to the end of his series with two more Christian-themed novels: *Peace Like a River* (1957), a novel about the desert-dwelling Christian ascetics of the fourth century; and *My Holy Satan* (1958), which displayed the cruelty and fanaticism of the Inquisition. Both novels would have deeply offended Christian readers if there had been any, but these volumes sold no better than the previous two. This left only one book to go, and, in 1960, Swallow published *Orphans in Gethsemane*, the fully revised story of Vridar Hunter, his early life in Idaho, his marriage to Neola and her suicide, and his irrepressible desire to become a writer. Fisher used the term *orphan* to describe all of the Vridar-types in the series. They had been deprived by their history of a mother-god, and they rejected the authority of the father-god, so they were spiritual orphans in a religion-soaked world.

At 987 pages, *Orphans in Gethsemane* was the longest book that Fisher ever wrote. Fisher guaranteed publication by putting up $4,000 of his own money to pay for printing costs. Swallow was hesitant to accept, but he ended up accepting it as a "joint venture" between the author and the publisher.[68] Fisher lost most of the money that he invested in *Orphans in Gethsemane*, but this was more than offset by the sale of the paperback rights to the entire series to Almat Publishing, the parent company of Pyramid Books, which had become famous for its lurid cover drawings and tantalizing blurbs. When Fisher's complex psychological novels appeared in paperback, they were presented with naked women on the covers and promises of "naked lust," "sex worship in a pagan society," and "blood lusts and animal passions."[69] The marketing ploy worked, and Fisher recorded 1961 revenues of more than $2,000 on sales of just one book in the series, *The Divine Passion*, which sold more than 110,000 paperback copies.[70]

With the *Testament of Man* complete, Vardis Fisher felt that he had done the work that he was supposed to do. Between 1960 and his death in 1968, he wrote and published only one more novel—the 1965 Western historical novel *Mountain Man*, which would become the basis for the Robert Redford movie *Jeremiah Johnson* and bring Fisher posthumous fame and fortune that rivaled the success of *Children of God*. He also wrote *Suicide or Murder* (1962), a nonfiction book about the death of Meriwether Lewis based on research that he conducted for *Tale of Valor*. And in February of 1968, Vardis and Opal published a guidebook that they wrote together called *Gold Rushes and Mining Camps of the Early American West.*

During these last years, Fisher settled into the role of local curmudgeon. He continued to write and syndicate editorial columns in Idaho newspapers. In his last years, he found common cause with his liberal academic friends like Alan Swallow in their joint opposition to the Vietnam War. And, right up until his death he continued attending writers' conferences, giving occasional speeches, and corresponding with the handful of young scholars who were writing their dissertations on his work. Just six months before his death he had been the writer-in-residence during the six-week Winter Session at the College of Idaho.[71]

On July 9, 1968, newspapers throughout Idaho and beyond reported that Vardis Fisher had died at the age of 73. They did not report how he died, and it took several more days for explanations to emerge. On July 12, the papers reported the results of an autopsy: "an overdose of sleeping pills combined with alcohol."[72] The manner of death immediately raised the question of whether it was an accidental overdose or an intentional suicide, with most people who knew Fisher strongly suspecting the latter. This suspicion appears to have been confirmed by a handwritten note from Opal that was not discovered until Fisher's oldest son, Grant, donated a large collection of family papers to Boise State University in 1997. "When the time came," she wrote, he walked deliberately to that door, forbidden by church and secular law, paused briefly to thumb his nose all around, opened the door with a key of seconal and gin, and strode out."[73]

Was Vardis Fisher a Mormon Writer?

As we have already seen, Vardis Fisher's connection to Mormonism has been fiercely contested. Well-meaning Mormon scholars such as Leonard Arrington and Jon Haupt did their best to fit Fisher in a Mormon box, while his much-aggrieved widow did her best to keep him out of it. Both Arrington and Haupt, on the one hand, and Opal Laurel Holmes on the other, were correct about some things and dead wrong about others. For example, "The Mormon Heritage of Vardis Fisher" claimed, very defensibly, that Fisher had strong cultural and historical ties to Mormonism and that these ties influenced much of what he wrote. But Arrington and Haupt went well beyond their evidence in asserting that Fisher never renounced

Mormonism (he did) or in speculating that, by the time of his death, he had softened on the religion of his youth (he had not).

But Holmes overstated her case, too. There is simply no way, looking at the objective evidence, to dismiss Fisher's connection to Mormonism as an insignificant part of his life or as a momentary lapse in his judgment. In her open letter to Spencer W. Kimball, Holmes states that "although Fisher's parents had been baptized into the Mormon Church as children, they did not practice the faith; and cared so little about Mormonism, that they never bothered to have their own children baptized."[74] As his own autobiographical writings make clear, though, Fisher's parents could not have had him baptized as a child because there was nobody around to do the baptizing. But they did raise him as a Mormon, and that shaped his life.

In a 2000 study of Fisher's Mormon heritage, BYU English professor Stephen L. Tanner referred to the Arrington-Holmes controversy and attempted to reconcile the two views by parsing the definition of "Mormonism." Tanner argues that Arrington and others are correct to call Fisher a "Mormon" to the extent that Mormonism is a "social-historical phenomenon." He had, Tanner argues, "a regional Mormon heritage in the way that a New Englander or a Southerner might have a regional heritage." But he did not have the experiences that would define someone as Mormon in more than a cultural sense. "To be so reared," he explains, "would typically mean that a boy began regular attendance in junior Sunday school at age four; be baptized at eight; be ordained to the Aaronic priesthood at twelve; serve in the offices of Deacon, Teacher. and Priest by age twenty; and then be ordained to the Melchizedek Priesthood." In this sense, he concludes, "Fisher was a complete outsider."[75]

The Mormon *cursus honorum* that Tanner describes here would apply perfectly to a male child born just about anywhere in the world in 1995. And it would apply reasonably well to one born in 1925 in the well-developed Mormon communities of the Wasatch Front. But these well-timed steps simply did not apply to Latter-day Saints living in rural isolation at the beginning of the last century. Both the institutional Church and the prevailing Mormon culture looked very different in the environment of Fisher's childhood. Much more of the indoctrination of children took place at home, and it was usually limited to an understanding of the Bible and the Book of Mormon and the prophetic mission of Joseph Smith. In Fisher's case, his sister reports, it also included regular readings by their father from the Doctrine & Covenants—a uniquely Mormon sacred text consisting of revelations recorded by Joseph Smith and other Church leaders.[76] All of which makes Vardis Fisher, as Mick McAllister has suggested, "the product of a fairly typical frontier Mormon upbringing."[77]

In the third book of the tetralogy, Fisher gives us a very apt metaphor for his Mormonism when his fictional alter ego, Vridar Hunter, has a conversation with a Jewish fraternity brother named Dave Roth. A deeply cynical man, Roth does not seem like the sort of person to join a fraternity, so the equally cynical Vridar asks him why he joined. "Being in a frat makes it easier for me to get along. I can go to some social flings," Roth responds. "Now and then a Christian smiles at me. And that . . . is quite a gift to a Jew." Vridar tries to protest that he is not himself religious—that he is not a Christian or a Mormon. But Roth stops him cold: "Yes you are. Religion is like smallpox. If you get a good dose you wear scars. You had a good dose." Vridar does not dispute the conclusion.[78]

Like Vridar Hunter, Vardis Fisher got a good dose of Mormonism. And like Vridar, he wore scars. He did not believe in, or adhere to, the doctrines of the LDS Church. He renounced and ridiculed those doctrines throughout his life. But his people were Mormon. His father, mother, sister, first wife, and two of his sons were active Latter-day Saints, and the stories and values that shaped his childhood were deeply rooted in the Mormon tradition—a fact that he acknowledged clearly just a year before his death in an interview with University of South Dakota English Professor John R. Milton. Fisher explained that his people "came across the plains with Brigham Young in the great Mormon exodus, because all my people on both sides then, as far as I know, were Mormons, and still are.[79]

Joseph M. Flora, the most prolific and important 20th-century literary scholar to study Vardis Fisher, believed that "Fisher's Mormonism ran deep." "It was not merely something that Fisher revolted against," Flora insists, "it was also something that helped form his life style and code."[80] Flora equated Fisher's Mormonism with James Joyce's Catholicism. Like Joyce, Fisher was profoundly influenced by the religion of his youth. Like Joyce, he renounced this religion and declared himself an atheist. And, like Joyce, he found it impossible to write and think without inhabiting the context of the religion he renounced. Much the same can be said of other writers associated with a religious heritage. Literary scholars have long been comfortable calling

Saul Bellow a "Jewish writer" and John Updike a "Protestant writer," without much concern about either man's beliefs or practices.

Whatever Fisher's feelings about the Church of Jesus Christ of Latter-day Saints were, Mormon religion shaped his values, and Mormon culture structured his understanding of himself and his world. As much as Fisher complained about the Mormon-saturated environment that he grew up in, he chose to return to that environment—after living in both Chicago and New York City—and to spend the rest of his life in places that the Mormons built. And, because Fisher had a greater stature with the Eastern literary establishment than any other Mormon writer of the first half of the 20th century, his framing of the Mormon experience has had profound implications for the way that Latter-day Saints have been portrayed in American literature since. These patterns of influence are important, and we can trace them in some detail. But we must first acknowledge that, while Vardis Fisher was not a faithful or believing member of the Church of Jesus Christ of Latter-day Saints, and while he was suspicious of and hostile to all varieties of religious belief, he was still—in ways that continue to matter—a Mormon writer.

CHAPTER TWO

Vardis Fisher and the Beginnings of Mormon Regionalism

Regional stories cannot be told only from the inside. While distinguishing between a region's "inside" and "outside" by this co-presence . . . analysis must include the outside. Notions that a culture's region represents the relatively unimpeded elaboration of a single group's culture within space are inadequate. The Mormon culture region cannot be fully understood if it is seen most fundamentally as the product of an evolving or maturing LDS culture.

—Ethan Yorgason, *The Transformation of the Mormon Culture Region*

Vardis Fisher appeared on the national literary scene at almost the same time as most of the other important regional writers of the 20th century. His first novel, *Toilers of the Hills*, was published in October of 1928, less than a year before the first novels by John Steinbeck, Thomas Wolfe, and Erskine Caldwell—and just a few months before the publication of *Sartoris*, the first of William Faulkner's novels set in the fictional Yoknapatawpha County.[1] In 1930, twelve well-known Southern writers joined together to write their regional manifesto: *I'll Take My Stand: The South and the Agrarian Tradition*, which helped to consolidate a new kind of literary regionalism that emerged in the 1920s. In the first decades of this intellectual movement, a new pack of writers with modernist sensibilities turned the raw narrative materials of their home cultures into works of literature that shook the world.

Like these other writers, Fisher began his career writing works of regional fiction. Or at least that was how reviewers and critics described them. Some of the earliest academic criticism of Fisher's work compared him to

Southern regionalists such as William Faulkner and Erskine Caldwell.[2] It was a natural comparison in some ways; all three novelists wrote about the rural, agrarian poor of their region. But in other ways it made no sense at all. By 1930, "the South" had been a coherent region for 200 years—longer even than there was a United States to be a part of. The Rocky Mountain West, on the other hand, was still forming at the time. As Ray B. West argued in his groundbreaking book *Writing in the Rocky Mountains* (1947), this was the last area of the country to be settled and the last to develop its own regional identities in literature. In fact, West argued, the only areas of the Rocky Mountains with the kind of coherent culture necessary to produce a regional literature in the 1930s were those settled by the Mormons. "Mormons," he insisted, "represented the single, early group of permanent settlers to come into the region already possessed of a single, unified belief, a cultural core against which the chaos of the frontier could be judged and set into some kind of order."[3]

West's view of literary history closely parallels the view of contemporary demographers and geographers who study "the Mormon culture region" as a discrete region within the Rocky Mountains. The term *Mormon culture region* was first used in the 1960s by Donald W. Meinig, who defined it as an area of the American West with "a *core* in the Wasatch Oasis, a *domain* over much of Utah and southeastern Idaho, and a *sphere* extending from eastern Oregon to Mexico." There is, Meinig concludes, "ample evidence that a distinctive Mormon culture is recognizable and important and that it is dominant over a large area in the Far West and that the Mormon region will long endure as a major pattern within the American West and thereby will continue to warrant far greater attention from American geographers."[4]

What does it mean to call a specific area of the country a "culture region" based on a religious affiliation that not everybody in the region shares? This becomes a central question in Ethan Yorgason's seminal 2003 book, *Transformation of the Mormon Culture Region*. To be a "region," he explains, an area must occupy roughly contiguous spaces on a map, but, even more importantly, it must occupy a position in the minds of the people who live in those spaces. A region is a region, ultimately, because the people on the inside understand that they belong to it—and the people on the outside acknowledge that they do as well. In this sense, the Mormon cultural region emerged when Mormons and non-Mormons in the area began to see themselves as a common culture. For more than 70 years, these two groups did not share enough cultural assumptions to support a joint regional identity. "By 1920," he explained, "Mormons and non-Mormons sensed that they shared a common regional destiny and that they could jointly call the region home."[5] Once this regional identity coalesced, Yorgason argues, a series of radical transformations in both the Church and the culture took shape as Mormonism and Western American culture began to influence each other.

The emergence of a coherent cultural sphere had consequences for literature from and about the region. Mormonism, of course, had long been the subject of bad fiction. In the hundred years after its founding in 1830, the Church of Jesus Christ of Latter-day Saints appeared in more than a hundred novels published in England or America, nearly all of which focused largely or entirely on Mormons kidnapping young women for their harems or sending Danite avengers to kill their enemies. Many of these came in the form of the dime novels, or (in England) penny dreadfuls—full novels printed on newsprint in agonizingly small type and sold for anywhere between five and 25 cents. At least 36 such novels have been identified in extant collections that treat Mormonism and Mormon characters—most sported titles like "Dolores the Danites Daughter" or "Secret Works in Salt Lake City."[6] Two of the more respectable novels in this kind—Arthur Conan Doyle's *A Study in Scarlett* (1887) and Zane Grey's *Riders of the Purple Sage*—each sold millions of copies and launched, respectively, the detective and hardback Western genres.

By the 1920s, historical fiction involving Mormons had settled into well-worn stereotypes based on nearly a hundred years of tradition. Mormons themselves pushed back with novels and stories of their own. Between 1895 and 1920, faithful Latter-day Saints in Utah published dozens of works of "Home Literature"—novels and other works of literature produced for Mormon audiences and either published in Church magazines or printed by the Church-owned *Deseret New Press*.[7] But as Mormons and non-Mormons coalesced into a single region—one partially defined, but not entirely circumscribed, by its dominant religion—neither the sensational caricatures nor the faith-promoting stories could contain the vitality of the resulting culture.

At the end of the decade, Vardis Fisher became the first major writer from the Mormon culture region to write about that region without falling into one or the other of these categories. His early Antelope novels were nothing like the faithful and affirming books of Nephi Anderson, but neither were

they *Riders of the Purple Sage*. They were realistic portrayals of the last generation of American pioneers—the people who settled the last wild places
on the continent while their fellow Americans were building skyscrapers
and mass-producing automobiles. The books are not about Mormonism
per se; but they are about the world that Mormon colonists created—and
many of their characters, including Fisher's alter ego Vridar Hunter, have
to determine their own position relative to the region's dominant religion.

Fisher's ambiguous relationship to Mormonism made him an ideal can-
didate to introduce the region's stories to the larger literary world. Success-
ful regionalist writing rarely comes from the center of a region's culture. It
requires one to inhabit a space that is simultaneously inside and outside
of the main cultural currents it describes. Fisher came from the region's
borderlands, both geographically (rural Idaho rather than Salt Lake City
or Provo), and ideologically (he was raised in the Mormon tradition but
no longer practiced the religion or accepted its beliefs). Whether or not we
should consider Fisher's early novels "Mormon literature" is a complicated
question that will ultimately depend on the definitions we employ. But
they were undoubtedly the first important regional novels to come from
the region defined by Mormon culture.

Fisher's Mormon Yoknapatawpha

Between 1928 and 1937, Vardis Fisher wrote seven novels set, in whole or
part, in the Antelope region of Southern Idaho. Four of the novels—*In
Tragic Life* (1932), *Passions Spin the Plot* (1934), *We Are Betrayed* (1935), and
No Villain Need Be (1936)—constitute an autobiographical tetralogy.[8] The
other three—*Toilers of the Hills* (1928), *Dark Bridwell* (1931), and *April: A
Fable of Love* (1937)—include the same settings and characters found in
the tetralogy but are not directly autobiographical.[9] To this body of work,
we can add six short stories published between 1933 and 1939, and a collection of ten character sketches in sonnet form—inspired by Edgar Lee
Masters's *Spoon River Anthology* (1915)—that were published in anthologies
and little magazines between 1928–1931.[10] The stories and poems are set in
the same world as the Antelope novels and often involve characters, or at
least families, from the other books.

Taken together, these novels, stories, and poems constitute a single fictional society much like Thomas Hardy's Wessex or William Faulkner's

28

Yoknapatawpha. Antelope is a coherent storyworld that shares characters, families, and even different perspectives on the same events. Unlike Hardy or Faulkner, however, Fisher writes himself into the story. Five of the seven novels revolve around the Hunter family—a thinly disguised version of the Fishers—and nearly all of the major events in these five novels correspond to events that occurred in Fisher's own family.

A comic scene in *April: A Fable of Love* gets to the heart of the way that Mormonism functions in the world of the Antelope novels. The main narrative of *April* explores the romantic adventures of June Weeg, "the homeliest girl in Antelope." June, who is 24 years old when the novel begins, longs to be "April," the vibrant, attractive version of herself that she has created in her mind. She has been raised on a steady diet of romantic novels and has a definite idea of what a good husband should be like. And he should not be like the man who has been courting her for years—a good-hearted but uneducated bachelor named Sol Incham. As Sol and June are destined to end up together, Fisher must establish Sol's worth. To do this, he creates a scene (Chapter 4 in the novel) in which Sol is proclaimed an ideal Mormon bishop—despite the fact that he is not a Mormon and does not believe in God.

As this scene begins, the Mormons in the community need somebody to become the new bishop of Antelope. Of the seventeen Mormon men in the community, however, not a single one of them meets the worthiness standards required of a bishop, as Amos Spoffard tells the community from the pulpit of the church:

> Now me . . . I chew tobacco and I ain't fit to be bishop. . . . I'm plumb ashamed of myself but that don't seem to help much. Now Brother Albert, if he'd stop chewun the filthy weed, he'd make us a good bishop. And Brother Ben, he uses snootch. And Brother Hans, he drinks coffee by the barrel. And Brother Will—he smokes and drinks. . . . Brother Charley—I guess he don't smoke or drink or chew but he cusses like the blue blazes.[11]

The assembly finally concludes that they will have to offer the position of bishop to a non-Mormon, since "everyone knows that the best persons in Antelope don't seem to believe in God." One of the men stands to nominate Sol, pointing out that, despite not believing in God, he is the best Christian in the community. Another member of the crowd points out that Sol constantly helps other people, bringing them groceries and chopping their firewood, and he is "the only person in antelope who lives the way Jesus told us to live."[12] The scene ends without Sol becoming bishop (Fisher clearly knew enough about the workings of the Church to know that such a thing could not happen), but the audience gets a good sense of how religion works in a frontier community far away from the center of the Church.

The comic situation in *April*—an atheist who almost becomes a Mormon bishop—has a tragic counterpart in "Charles North," one of the Antelope sonnets that Fisher published in 1929. Charles North is a Mormon bishop who does not believe in God, or, at least, is not sure that he believes in God, despite the fact that a heavy ecclesiastical responsibility has been thrust upon him:

> He was a bishop, and he made to God
> Some small concessions while his conscience purred
> He prayed—and doubted that God ever heard.
> And half surmised that heaven was a fraud.
> Its ruler, said he, was a trifle odd,
> And much of what he did was too absurd;
> But on the road that piety has trod,
> Charles was a titan, impotent, and spurred.
> His tenure ended and he laid aside
> His robe of office as he would a coat.
> Religion now became an anecdote
> And conscience an expatriated guide;
> Until at last among the Ravagers,
> A shape smiled grimly and removed his spurs.

In a series of five sonnets, Fisher explores the consequences of North's dedication to a religion he does not believe in for his family: his wife, "Lizzie North," detests her enforced role as a homemaker and either neglects or abuses their children; one of their children, "Baby North," died as an infant; another, "Jess North," is profoundly mentally disabled; and a third, "Sally North," commits suicide.[13]

In a society peopled by both the Mormon Charles North and the non-Mormon Sol Incham, Mormonism functions as a defining cultural force in ways not always connected to religion or personal belief. The world of these novels is fundamentally Mormon, but not in ways that most modern readers will recognize. As Dale Morgan wrote in his 1942 essay "Mormon Storytellers," Fisher's early Mormon characters "are the legitimate offspring of the Mormons who saw glories in the sky and praised God for a latter-day Prophet, but Dock Hunter is the product of the interaction of Mormon society with the desert environment."[14] These characters are for the most part ruthless pragmatists who focus intensely on wrenching survival from a hostile soil. They think of God only occasionally, and not always with affection, and their Mormonism is a matter of habit and custom more than choice or devotion.

But Fisher makes it very clear that the inhabitants of Antelope are pioneers and that they came to Southern Idaho as a direct expression of their Mormon pioneer heritage. "It was the habit of Brigham Young to send settlers out in all directions," he told John R. Milton in a 1967 interview. "My father and one of his brothers were two of a small colony sent to the Upper Snake River Valley."[15] These two brothers, Joseph Oliver and Alma Lehi Fisher, were part of a group of Mormon settlers tasked in 1879 with settling Southeastern Idaho. Once the frontier community of Annis was firmly established, the two Fisher Brothers struck out on their own to become a third generation of pioneers in even more remote frontiers. Alma, who was known by his nickname "Doc," went further into the wilderness to settle in the Antelope Hills. Joe moved to a forty-acre farm that he purchased along an uninhabited stretch of the Snake River. Their experiences formed the backbone of Fisher's Antelope novels.

In a 1937 essay titled "The Strange Case of Vardis Fisher," American critic John Peale Bishop suggested that the great value of Antelope novels lay in the fact that Fisher himself had been a witness to the very tail end of the pioneer era. "We are conscious in those . . . novels of Vardis Fisher that are laid entirely in the Idaho benchland, that the whole pioneer movement has come to a dead end; its exhaustion has left these people depleted; morally and emotionally, it still runs its course." Peale, an arch-Modernist, saw Fisher's novels as a clear distillation of a deep problem in the American psyche: for a hundred and fifty years, Americans built an image of themselves around an ever-expanding frontier. Now that "the space of the American continent has been conquered," there is no West for young men to go to, yet; for very deep-seated reasons, "these Idahoans are still held by the example of their fathers; they cannot stop, but must forever be making a fresh start. . . . Courage and hope, those two most admirable virtues of the frontiersman, have become in this late and unpromising land, cruelly meaningless."[16]

Vardis Fisher was never a romantic, but neither did he share Bishop's modernist despair. What was important to him about the pioneer spirit of his ancestors was not the exploration of new places or the finding of new frontiers. It was the holy power of hard work to wrest a living out of the most hostile of environments—the ability to come to a desert and, through toil and sacrifice, make it blossom as a rose.[17] This is the theme of one of his early Antelope sonnets, "Joe Hunter," who, we will later learn in the tetralogy, is based on Vardis's own father, Joseph Fisher:

> Time built a pioneer and set him down
> Upon the grayest waste of Idaho.
> He clubbed the desert and he made it grow
> In broad and undulating fields of brown.
> He laid his might upon it, stripped its frown
> Of drought and thistles; till by sweat and glow
> He left the aged and barren hills aglow
> With color—and its flame was his renown.
> He poured his great dream into golden wheat;
> Until his gnarled and calloused hands had wrought
> A deep and quiet holiness of work.[18]

The phrase "clubbed the desert and made it grow" is perhaps a little more energetic than "made the desert blossom as a rose." But the meaning is the same, as is the fundamental moral value behind both the novel about the author's uncle and the poem about his father, beautifully summed up in the line "a deep and quiet holiness of work." This is a constant theme in Fisher's work, and in his life—not just that hard work pays off, or is morally efficacious, but that hard work can turn something barren into something beautiful.

"The deep and quiet holiness of work"

The first of the Antelope novels, *Toilers of the Hills*, tells the story of Dock and Opal Hunter—characters based on Fisher's uncle and aunt, Doc and Martha Fisher, who were among the first to apply dry-farming techniques to wheat crops in rural Idaho. By his own account, Fisher wrote *Toilers of the Hills* "after reading the romantic foolishness of Willa Cather."[19] Fisher's novel eschews romanticism for the conventions of literary naturalism, in which ultimately insignificant people struggle against immense forces that they can neither understand nor control.

Dock and Opal come to Antelope and are continually defeated by the land, which does not produce enough rainfall to sustain a farm. They have a large family of eight children and live much of their lives near starvation in a two-room shack that Dock built on the top of a mountain. Though Dock is the main character of the novel, his wife, Opal, is the viewpoint character through whom the story is processed. Opal hates the isolation that she experiences in Antelope and stays with Dock only from loyalty and a strong sense of family. She is, therefore, a perfect skeptical audience to judge the success or failure of Dock's life. To Opal, Dock constantly asserts that he can tame the land. "I aim to conquer this-here place or I aim to die," he tells his cousin, whose child was stillborn during an unendurably cold winter. "God give a man ways to conquer it if he'll only find them."[20]

Dock does find them. Through hard work, intuition, and a lot of trial and error, he uncovers the secrets of dry farming and begins to produce lucrative crops. The family remains together, despite extreme hardships and Dock's occasional outbreaks of cruelty. More settlers come to Antelope and, at the end of the novel, Dock builds Opal the new house she has always wanted and they live in a functional frontier community. In the final pages, both Dock and Opal realize that, in spite of all their hardships, they have lived a good life. "You said we'd starve, and I knowed we wouldn't," Dock tells Opal after they bring a bumper wheat crop to market. "It's to keep fightun makes a man win, just to keep fightun and never say die. You said I was a worseless dreamer, and it's dreamers keeps the old world on its legs."[21]

Dock Hunter, a descendent of the first Mormon pioneers in the Great Basin, shares their faith in furious industry. Much as *Toilers of the Hills* celebrates the virtue of industry, Fisher's next novel, *Dark Bridwell*, condemns the vice of indolence. Both novels are set in the Antelope Hills between the end of the nineteenth century and the outbreak of World War I, and both revolve around men who move their families to the rugged isolation of rural Idaho. But Charley Bridwell, the central character of *Dark Bridwell*, is as unlike Dock Hunter as any man could be. Where Dock is industrious and reserved, Charley is lazy and effusive. Dock moves to Antelope to tame the land, and he is willing to exist at a mere sustenance level until he does so. Charley comes because he knows he can find a way to live at a mere sustenance level with only a few hours of work a week. The Bridwells' closest neighbor is Dock Hunter's brother Joe, who is modeled on Fisher's own father. And Joe's son Vridar, who will have the starring role in the tetralogy, plays a supporting role in *Dark Bridwell*.

The Hunters and the Bridwells form a crucial opposition in all of Fisher's Antelope fiction. The Hunters—Dock, Joe, and Vridar—are hardworking, conscientious, and at least nominally, Mormon. They bring a civilizing impulse to the wilderness. Charley Bridwell has only contempt for this way of looking at the world:

> Joe gave his flesh and bone to the grubbing-out of all manner of tangled brush that covered his land. He worked from five in the morning until ten at night, seldom missing either a Sunday or a holiday. He slaved endlessly, until his body was bent and his hands gnarled, and his mind twisted like the dollar sign; and what would he ever get from his labor, save a little pile of money and a larger patch of lucerne . . . ? He was, for Charley, a symbol of the stupidity and folly of life."[22]

Charley Bridwell and his family are creatures of the wild who live an almost prehistoric life. Charley hunts and fishes, gathers fruits and berries, does odd jobs, steals other people's cattle, and begs and borrows from his friends—leaving most of his days free for contemplation and juvenile mischief, which on more than one occasion turns into outright cruelty. Jed, the oldest Bridwell child, inherits all of his father's cruelty but none of his good nature. As a very young child, Jed develops a homicidal hatred for his father that grows until he leaves home at 15 to pursue the girl responsible for his sexual initiation. Charley and Jed are, respectively, the viewpoint characters of the first two sections of *Dark Bridwell*.

The third and most tragic portion of the story is told from the perspective of Lela, Charley's wife, who genuinely loves her husband but resents the solitude that he has imposed on her. From early on the reader knows that Charley's primary motivation in moving to Antelope was to isolate Lela "because he was afraid she would leave him, afraid she would tire of his lazy or drunken hours."[23] By design, Antelope becomes her prison. Indeed, Fisher may have derived the name "Bridwell" from the London woman's prison, Bridewell, that was featured prominently in much of the literature he studied as a PhD student in English. This would make the novel's title "Dark Bridwell" a tragic pun where Lela is concerned. Much like Opal Hunter, Lela endures her prison loyally for more than 20 years, as nearly all of her children fall prey to Charley's inexplicable cruel streak. When she discovers that Charley has been teaching their youngest son to curse and chew tobacco, Lela turns against Charley for good. When Jed returns to have it out with his father, Lela attacks her husband and leaves with her remaining children—and no Bridwell is ever heard from again.

First positively, and then negatively, the first two Antelope novels make an argument for the moral value of hard work. It was also a core value for Vardis Fisher. In the essay "The Novelist and His Work," first published in 1949, Fisher describes his typical work routine as follows: "When I am working on a book . . . I stick to an inflexible routine, seven days a week, month after month, until the first draft is completed." He explains that he writes for between two and four hours each morning and then "I go outside for three or four hours of heavy labor—and I do mean heavy labor. We live in the Idaho country. Ten years ago we bought a few acres of wasteland . . . which the owner had abandoned as worthless." Fisher's explanation of what his hard labor accomplished over ten years brims with the pride of his pioneer ancestors:

> Our ten years here have been ten years of hard labor. We have built our own house, such as it is, including the masonry, wiring and plumbing; erected five other buildings; and planted several thousand trees, including pine, spruce, juniper, and other evergreens. I have constructed a dam and screens around one side of the lake and have it stocked with rainbow trout. I have built concrete walks and head-gates and walls; dug ditches and made fences; laid a lot of pipeline to irrigate our trees; and in various other ways have been a son of toil—so much so indeed that some of the good folk of the valley have long been distressed by my ordinary appearance. They think that a writer should look the part.[24]

Hard work has been extolled by people of all religions for thousands of years. But the combination of hard work and pioneering an arid landscape has deep connections to the pioneer culture of Utah and the Mormon culture region. This is why the beehive is the most important symbol in the state of Utah, often accompanied by the one-word state motto: "Industry." It would be almost impossible to imagine a serious regional fiction from this culture that did not somehow embody a sense of pioneering, conquering the desert, and "a deep and quiet holiness of work."

Prophets and Puritans

The tetralogy is a fictionalized version of Fisher's own life set in the fictional world of *Toilers of the Hills* and *Dark Bridwell*. Together, the four novels tell the story of Vridar Hunter, Fisher's alter ego, from his birth in Annis, Idaho, through his return to Idaho in his mid-30s after giving up a university teaching career. The central event of the novels is the suicide of Neola Hunter, Vridar's first wife, who kills herself in response to his infidelities at the end of *We Are Betrayed*—just as Fisher's first wife, Leona, did in 1924. The tetralogy parallels the psychological narrative of a very different work that was a subject of Fisher's dissertation: George Meredith's *Modern Love*, a sequence of 50 sixteen-line sonnets detailing the dissolution of his own unhappy marriage. The titles of all four novels in the tetralogy—*In Tragic Life*, *Passions Spin the Plot*, *We Are Betrayed*, and *No Villain Need Be*—come directly from the closing lines of the 43rd sonnet in *Modern Love*:

> This morning: but no morning can restore
> What we have forfeited. I see no sin:
> The wrong is mix'd. In tragic life, God wot,
> No villain need be! Passions spin the plot:
> We are betray'd by what is false within.

Like Meredith (whose wife, rather than he, was the unfaithful partner), Fisher wants to narrate the failure of his marriage as a tragedy. These lines, which he includes as an epigraph to each of the four novels, do just that. They lay the blame on fate and circumstance—and on "passions" that, by their very nature, cannot be controlled and do not require a villain. The final line of the sonnet—"we are betrayed by what is false within"—became Fisher's rallying cry for the tetralogy, which he imagined as a project of confessional truth-telling and personal authenticity. But it was also a work of exorcism conceived at a time when Fisher's guilt was so overwhelming that he contemplated taking his own life.[25]

We cannot automatically assume that everything that Fisher ascribes to Vridar Hunter is an autobiographical detail from his own life. Characters in novels must always be read primarily as characters in novels, who work on different principles than actual human beings do. The events in the tetralogy do not map perfectly onto the life events of its author. Fisher collapses some historical occasions together, ignores large swaths of his life, and invents specific events that help him focus narrative threads. Nonetheless, these four novels, as Fisher acknowledged himself in a 1942 article about the tetralogy, "make obvious and extensive use of very personal experiences," though he also insists that "all novels are autobiographical for those who know how to read."[26]

The first volume of the tetralogy, *In Tragic Life*, narrates Vridar Hunter's life from his birth to the moment he leaves high school—and Mormonism—to strike out on his own. Religion is not a local-color detail in this book, as it is in *April* and some of the other Antelope novels. Religious themes pervade the novel, from Vridar's auspicious birth—which is soaked in religious significance for his superstitious Mormon relatives—to the final page of the novel, when Vridar decides not to serve an LDS mission and, instead, renounces all religion and strikes out on his own. The entire novel can be read as a spiritual autobiography in the tradition of John Bunyan's *Grace Abounding to the Chief of Sinners*—though in Fisher's case, grace does very little abounding, and the protagonist ultimately decides that there is no such thing as sin.

But this discovery comes very late in the novel. For most of his childhood and adolescence, Vridar is ruled by two overwhelming religious beliefs that he inherits from his Mormon parents: First, he believes that he has been chosen by God to be a prophet and to accomplish some great spiritual work. Second, much like Bunyan, he believes that he is a terrible sinner who must earn his salvation through profound self-sacrifice. These two beliefs combine to propel him, in the novel's final chapters, to fully embrace Mormonism and then to fully reject it.

The Vridar-as-prophet motif begins with his birth. When he is born with a caul, his paternal grandmother predicts that he will be a prophet, "for Joseph Smith, she had been told, was born with a veil over his face." Later, the narrative reports, this prophecy became a family legend "until it imposed a profound and unhappy influence on the child's life."[27] As Vridar grows up, he is obsessed with the idea that he is destined to fulfill a great religious calling. At eight, he begins reading the Bible and announces to his mother that he wants to be a prophet when he grows up. "Yes, he would be a prophet, a voice of doom from the heights. He would talk with God; and then he would go forth, speaking with a tongue of fire. Snake River would be smitten into seven streams; and all the Babylon's of earth would wither under his sword."[28]

These ideas continued to dominate his life. When he is nine, he begins to suffer from nightmares, which he interprets as Job-like tests of his fitness. "He became convinced in this year that he, like John the Baptist and Joseph Smith, was to be a prophet of God," and he goes out in the wilderness to seek a vision, which he in fact receives:

He saw a glorious vision. The heavens opened and he looked in; and saw, against a background of red and white clouds, a great lamb that stared at him, and the lamb had seven eyes and seven tails. Roundabout the lamb was a mist of white angels, and among these was a throne, and upon this throne sat a white god. He heard, then, a roaring like that of water, and thunder rolled out of the west, and behind it came four horses, one red and one black, one green and one blue. . . . The four beasts ran up to the throne, screaming like a horse in agony, and knelt in prayer upon the cloud-carpet of heaven. Hail began to fall, and it was like frozen blood; it dripped upon trees and withered them; and red streams flowed upon chaos.[29]

Vridar continues to believe in his own prophetic destiny well into his teen years. When his neighbor Jed Bridwell attacks him and starts to beat him senseless, he announces, "I'm to be a prophet" and demands, "so now you leave me alone."[30] And when he is called on a mission for the LDS Church after graduating from high school, he makes a list of "pros" and "cons" to accepting the call. Among the reasons that he should go on a mission, he lists "because I may be a prophet."[31] Even in the third volume of the tetralogy, after he has left the Church and is living in Chicago with his still-Mormon wife, Vridar announces that he still considers himself a prophet. "I no longer believe in the saint-and-sugar-beet doctrines of Mormonism," he tells his wife during an argument about religion. "And some day, Neola, I am going to write a book about all this. I'll show the cockeyed world of a prophet in the making."[32]

Prophets haunted Fisher throughout his career. In his adult life, he no longer wanted to be a prophet in the sense of a person who talks with God. But even as an atheist, he continued to feel called on to bring forth a new secular scripture—the *Testament of Man*, which would reframe the two testaments of the Bible as part of the human tendency to avoid the serious self-scrutiny that the advancement of civilization requires. Several of these novels revolve around prophet figures—normally portrayed negatively—who bend their societies toward the sterile, self-denying ideology that Fisher called "Puritanism" and associated with all religions, especially Mormonism. The major thing that prophets were against, at least in Fisher's mind, was sex. And the main thing they were for was guilt—which is also the second pillar of Vridar Hunter's religious experience in *In Tragic Life*.

Vridar learns from a very young age that God hates people who think about sex. His mother, Prudence Hunter, he pointed out, "had been taught by a stern and unrelenting mother that sexual passion was base and unclean." "Sex, for her," Fisher wrote was an unlovely necessity, an impure prelude to birth, and the most amazing of all the dark blunders of God."[33] Vridar grows up believing that sex is disgusting, that bodies are evil, and that intimacy of any kind will lead to his spiritual and physical destruction. When he becomes sexually curious and persuades his sister to take off her clothes, his mother finds out and tells him, "It's for things like that God sends people to hell. If you ever do things like that again, if you even think such things, God will never forgive you." From this, and several similar episodes, Vridar learns "a ghastly dread of the beautiful, the sweet, and the unexplained. Nothing was right, nothing was godly, except pain and solitude and hard ways."[34]

A turning point in the novel comes when Vridar is twelve, and one of his friends introduces him to masturbation, which he begins to practice regularly with a mixture of great pleasure and "deep guilt."[35] In time, the guilt begins to overwhelm him. "He had debased himself, sold his birthright," he tells himself. "He was doomed." He tries to regain his chosen status by "renouncing all joy and by scourging himself. . . . All thoughts of women, of feasting and revelry, he tried to bury with darkness; and thrice every day he fell to his knees in prayer." Despite his efforts, though, "he was drawn to the path of pleasure." So he continues to torment himself with a deep conviction of his sinful nature.[36]

Vridar's crisis of conscience comes when he is attending high school in Rigby and encounters a Victorian-era anti-masturbation pamphlet with the headline, WILL YOUR BRAIN ROT? After reading it, he experiences such deep guilt and hopelessness that he seeks out and begins attending the local Mormon Church. After only a few weeks of regular attendance, "he went, on a Sunday morning, to the cold waters of a canal and was shoved under; and he strode home, wondering if all his sin had been washed away."[37]

Soon after his baptism, however, Vridar begins to feel alienated by the Church he has joined. "The more he heard his teacher expound racial intolerance or speak of God's chosen people or reduce parable to plain arithmetic, the more he sickened and turned away."[38] A week after he decides to stop going to church, Vridar receives a call to serve a mission in Spain. This produces another crisis, which is exacerbated when his father tells him he cannot go, and his mother tells him he must. After agonizing and praying about the decision, Vridar decides to go—primarily because he thinks it is the only way he can ever be free of the grievous sin of masturbation.[39] For a brief time, it looks as though the two religious pillars of Vridar's life—his conception of himself as a chosen servant of God and his conviction that he has sinned grievously and needs to be redeemed—will come together in the call to serve a mission.

However, a chance encounter with one of his high school teachers, a committed freethinker named George Albert Turner, changes his mind. When Turner asks why he is going on a mission, Vridar simply says, "I—I've sinned." Turner laughs heartily and then delivers a passionate sermon on the nonexistence of sin. "Everything was beautiful," he said. "Everything, except the unimportant decay of death, was sweet and clean. The only sin was turning your back on life; the only religion lay in accepting life honestly and strongly, instead of ducking into a Church to pray." The power of these words shakes Vridar to the core, and he resolves not to serve a mission or ever return to Church again. Rather, he vows, he will "fight and fight until I can laugh, too, and be glad." And with this solemn vow, the first novel of the tetralogy ends.[40]

From the perspective of regional literature, it makes little difference whether Vridar Hunter—or Vardis Fisher for that matter—accepts or rejects the Mormon religion. What matters is that Fisher wrote a novel depicting Mormonism as the sort of thing that a literary character needs to have an opinion about—needs to accept or reject or otherwise have some position in relation to. Fisher's Antelope novels are the first American works of fiction of any consequence in which this is the case. This signaled two things to the world: 1) that Mormonism, which had been portrayed in literature almost entirely as a historical phenomenon, was a cultural force that shaped people's lives in the present; and 2) that the people whose lives had somehow been shaped by the Mormon faith were now developing a regional literature of their own.

CHAPTER THREE

Children of God and the Golden Age of Mormon Literature

Here was a story which I had known all my life, which I knew better than any other in American history. It held as much as any novelist could ask of farce and tragedy, melodrama, aspiration, violence, ecstasy— the strongest passions of mankind at white heat; the Kingdom of God and mob cruelty and martyrdom; bigotry and superstition and delusion; mystical exal- tation and the purity of faith; ambition and its over- throw, persecution and social revolt—all bound up . . . with the sweep of a full century of American life.

—Bernard DeVoto

In 1938, Utah-born novelist and historian Bernard DeVoto used his monthly column in *Harper's* magazine to ponder the possibility of writing an epic novel about the Mormon migration. A self-described "child of a Catho- lic father and a Mormon mother," DeVoto moved easily between the two religions, though his own upbringing was Catholic.[1] He wrote about Mor- monism in his nonfiction work *The Year of Decision: 1846* (1943), which treated the Mormon migration as one of several important instances of exploration and colonization in one crucial year of America's history. But, he concluded, neither he nor anybody else has enough talent to turn the story of Mormonism into first-rate fiction. "God is the best dramatist," he conceded. "I will content myself with less aspiring failures, leaving to more stubborn men the crash that any man must make who tries to compose fiction out of Joseph Smith and the Mormon people."[2]

In September of 1938, one month before DeVoto published this essay in *Harper's* magazine, Vardis Fisher signed a contract with that magazine's parent company to publish an epic novel of the Mormon migration that he had not yet given a title, but that he referred to in his correspondence as "the Mormon Book." Several other Eastern publishing houses expressed an interest in the book, and Fisher's agent, Elizabeth Nowell, found herself in the unfamiliar position of entertaining multiple offers for a book that had not even been finished.[3] Nowell pushed Fisher to accept an offer from Harper & Brothers on the understanding that, if it were published in 1939, the book would be a strong contender for the Harper Prize—a $7,500 publication award from the firm and the richest literary prize in the country at the time—which would virtually guarantee that the book would become a best seller.

Later in his career, Fisher dismissed both the Harper Prize and the novel that won it as inferior work. "Do literary prizes mean any more nowadays than a radio-give-away?" he asked in his 1953 book *God or Caesar?* "Not much," he answered. "I received a Harper Award for one of the poorest novels I have written."[4] When he was submitting his novel to *Harper's* in hopes of winning the prize, however, he saw it as his breakthrough novel and the Harper Prize as his best chance to launch himself into the ranks of major American writers. In a letter to Alfred Knopf pitching the book, he wrote that his "Mormon novel" was "the crucial novel of my career. During the fifteen years I've prepared for the writing of it, I've known it would be."[5]

For months after signing with Harper Brothers, Fisher fretted that he had no chance of winning the Harper Prize because one of the announced judges was Bernard DeVoto, who had already declared that nobody could make a great novel "out of Joseph Smith and the Mormon people." After this column came out, Fisher wrote to Nowell that "it will be more philosophic for you and me to forget about prizes and realize that one is awfully damned remote."[6] And yet DeVoto continued to loom large in Fisher's mind during the final stages of writing and revising the Mormon book. When Nowell sent him a list of proposed revisions that he found historically suspect, he retorted, "if you're after that prize, remember that some of your suggestions are precisely the kind that will make DeVoto look down his nose and spit."[7] And when he acknowledged several minor continuity errors, he worried that "a few persons like DeVoto who know something about Mormon history might Jump down my neck over such trivial matters."[8] In the end, DeVoto was replaced on the judging panel by Carl Van Doren, the well-known critic and historian who won a Pulitzer Prize for his biography of Benjamin Franklin. Van Doren was joined by two Pulitzer

Prize-winning novelists—Josephine Johnson and Louis Bromfield—to form the final judging panel for the 1939–40 Harper Prize.[9]

In June of 1939, two months before its publication, Harper & Brothers announced that *Children of God* by Vardis Fisher would be awarded its biannual prize. When the novel was published in August, it was accompanied by a full front-page review in the *New York Times Review of Books*. The reviewer, Fred T. Marsh, heaped unqualified praise upon Fisher's work. "Never has the Mormon story been done with anything like this subtlety and bigness," Marsh enthused. "It's a labor of love; it's a labor growing out of man's past and home and background; it's a labor of careful research." Even Bernard DeVoto praised it and declared himself a false prophet in his overwhelmingly positive review of Fisher's novel.[10] In September of 1939, *Children of God* climbed to #2 on the *Times* best-seller list—behind only John Steinbeck's *Grapes of Wrath*, one of the best-selling novels of the decade.

Prophets as Epic Heroes

Most of the Mormon migration novels of the 1930s used the standard historical-novel convention of telling the story from the perspective of fictional main characters and relegating historical figures to minor roles. Fisher does not adopt this convention until the third and final part of *Children of God*. The first two parts are narrated through the eyes of, respectively, Joseph Smith and Brigham Young. This narrative strategy presented Fisher with several risks that could have sunk the novel. First, it required him to compete with history in precisely the way that DeVoto claimed could not be done. Mormonism's first two prophets were huge, complicated, contradictory personalities who both left behind troves of writings and speeches in their own words. Fisher had to capture the essence of these oversized characters in a limited number of pages without running afoul of the historical record. And he knew too well that other people—specifically DeVoto—would be ready to pounce on anything that he got wrong.

By turning prophets into literary characters, Fisher also limited his ability to remain neutral on the epistemological questions that were sharply contested in his culture—and even in his own family. A novelist telling the story of Joseph Smith's First Vision through the eyes of a fictional minor character can bracket the question of whether or not God and Jesus Christ actually appeared to the young prophet and focus entirely on the responses of others. But when Joseph Smith himself is the main character, the novelist has to take a side: Did a fourteen-year-old boy really see God and Jesus Christ, or was he an attention-seeking liar or a deluded child? Were there really golden plates? Did an angel named Moroni actually appear to Joseph? Did the Three Witnesses really witness something? Fisher's own plan for *Children of God* made it virtually impossible for him to avoid taking firm positions on these questions—even though he knew that any firm position would alienate some portion of his potential audience.

Fisher, with the contrarian spirit that he demonstrated throughout his career, answered these questions in ways that managed to alienate almost everybody—or at least everybody with an extreme position either for or against Mormon truth claims. Fisher's Joseph Smith really does have a vision in which God and Jesus Christ appear and speak to him, and, with only a few exceptions, he tells the story the way that it appears in the LDS Pearl of Great Price.[11] But he also adds that Joseph "had been unclean with his own flesh" and that he felt deep guilt about it—guilt that propelled him to seek a vision from God to assure himself that he would not be damned for all of eternity.[12] This passage of *Children of God* has special significance for readers of *In Tragic Life*, the first book of the tetralogy, where Fisher's alter ego Vridar Hunter also struggles with masturbation and also sees a vision that is presented to readers as a fact—even as the narrative makes clear that it is the benign delusion of an extremely sensitive child who sincerely believes himself to be a prophet in the mold of Joseph Smith.[13]

"Benign delusion" largely sums up Fisher's attitude toward Smith in *Children of God*. Fisher presents Joseph as a poet and religious mystic who has a powerful spiritual vision that he can communicate to others only by setting it in a material frame. For example, when he tells his family about golden plates explaining the history of the Indians, which he saw only with his spiritual eyes, his brother Hyrum presses to know whether or not the plates actually existed, and "the incredulity in his brother's voice impelled [Joseph] to make one of the gravest mistakes of his life. He knew well that he had seen the plates only in a vision, but he felt nobody would believe that. . . . The only thought in his mind was this, that nobody would believe in golden plates if they were not tangible objects that could be measured and weighed."[14]

Fisher's Joseph Smith is not a hypocrite or a deceiver. He is "a philosopher with the soul of a monk."[15] Along with a keen mind and an active imagination, he has an absolute ability to convince himself that every idea he has comes directly from God. And yet, within these assumptions, Fisher treats Joseph much more softly than most other writers of the day. He contextualizes Nauvoo polygamy as a revelation sought partly because there were "more women than men in some of these communities and Joseph wondered what to do with them."[16] In explaining the Kirtland bank failure, Fisher portrays Joseph as a near ascetic who is so concerned with spiritual matters that he can't be bothered with filthy lucre. When Brigham Young tells him that the bank is failing and the people will be in rags, Joseph says only, "rags on human bodies are no disgrace, Brigham, if God is in their hearts."[17] And Fisher completely absolves Joseph of any complicity with the Danites or other Mormon vigilantes.[18]

Fisher's Joseph Smith is a tragic hero in the classical mode. He is good and noble, but also flawed, and his flaws eventually come to dominate his personality and lead to his demise. The catalyst for Joseph's downfall is plural marriage, which he introduces into the Nauvoo Mormon community near the end of "Morning," the first part of *Children of God*. It comes as the culmination of three different subplots that Fisher develops throughout this section:

> Month by month, as he came into power and peace, as he saw his city grow and his military organization take form, he thought of the advantage in the next life for those who had many offspring. He needed many wives—and many children if in the next world he was to advance rapidly toward godhood; because power there was determined by the number of progeny, as well as by righteous living in this world. He remembered again that God had peopled this planet and was still siring the millions of souls that came to human birth. There were other reasons no less urgent. In Nauvoo were more women than men, and Joseph abhorred prostitutes. If a woman had no husband, she would probably seek a lover and fall into abominable adultery; or she would sell herself in the brothels. He wanted no harlots in this city. Another reason, he admitted, with a wry smile for himself, was his appetite: he had never looked at a beautiful woman without wishing to touch her. This he had formerly regarded as a weakness of his flesh; but now he felt that God had planned for him to have many wives, and the more he considered the matter, the more certain his conviction became.[19]

Each of the justifications for polygamy that Fisher attributes to Joseph Smith in this passage comes from a different part of the historical record.

The theological argument that men should take multiple wives because spiritual power in the afterlife "was determined by the number of progeny" comes from mid-19th-century Mormon doctrine as articulated by Brigham Young, Heber C. Kimball, Orson Hyde, and other polygamous leaders. The argument that polygamy was necessary because of an imbalance between men and women came much later, largely as a retroactive (and inaccurate) justification for the practice by Mormons who no longer practiced or sanctioned it.[20] And the characterization of Smith's embrace of polygamy as a simple manifestation of his lustful nature lies at the heart of anti-Mormon critiques and non-Mormon explanations both past and present.

By weaving these three explanations for polygamy into a single characterization of Joseph Smith, Fisher telegraphs something about his approach to Mormon history in *Children of God*: when dealing with controversial issues, he often tries to synthesize contradictions into a narrative capable of containing both spiritual and material answers to the same questions. Joseph Smith was both a prophet and a fraud. The Book of Mormon is both history and fiction. Plural marriage was about becoming like God, taking care of extra women, and satisfying male libidos. Fisher rarely takes a side when he can figure out how to be on both sides of a question at the same time.

In the second part of the book, "Noon," the point of view shifts from Joseph Smith to Brigham Young who, true to form, Fisher portrays as both a cruel despot and an inspired leader. But Brigham is not a tragic figure. He is an epic hero like Gilgamesh or Aeneas—deeply flawed, larger-than-life figures who both create and embody their culture's understanding of ideal humanity. Brigham is the one truly vital character in *Children of God*—the person who manages to take the spiritual vision of Joseph Smith and do the hard work necessary to give that vision a material reality. Under his commanding, pragmatic leadership, the Church moves into the desert and colonizes large swaths of the West. Whereas Joseph Smith failed to build a lasting city, Brigham Young builds an empire.

In the process, he does some decidedly unprophetic things. One of the minor characters in the novel is Bill Hickman, one of Brigham Young's companions during the exodus whose memoir was published in 1872 with the lurid title, *Brigham's Destroying Angel: Being the Life, Confession, and Startling Disclosures of the Notorious Bill Hickman, the Danite Chief of Utah.*[21] The publisher, J. H. Beadle, was well known for publishing scandalous books about the Mormons, and contemporary historians do not consider the book to be a reliable primary source.[22] But Fisher read and absorbed the book and spared it the skeptical eye that he cast on almost every other source that he used. Fisher presents Hickman as Brigham Young's assassin, who takes the merest word from his leader as a mandate to kill, in God's name, those who threaten the Church. To his credit, Brigham does not abuse the arrangement—everyone that Hickman kills really does seem to represent a tangible threat to the well-being of the Saints. But as Fisher well knew, most Latter-day Saints would react very negatively to the image of their second prophet ordering assassinations, however necessary or justified.

But Fisher's Brigham Young is not merely a thug or a theocrat. He is by far the most complex and, ultimately, heroic character in *Children of God*. Unlike Smith, who had a spiritual vision for his people, Young had a social vision—one tethered firmly to the current world. Religion for Joseph was an end; for Brigham it was a means for creating an ideal society:

> Through it all, awake and asleep, Brigham was impelled by a great vision. He felt that this journey fed from the eager and searching millenniums in the remote background of human striving: it was more than desperate flight from enemies: it was a pilgrimage toward freedom, toward a fuller and richer destiny for the entire human race. In all that struggle for perfection and peace that had been the heritage of humanity for centuries. He was fighting for a society that would be charitable and righteous and free.[23]

Fisher saw the early Mormon experiments with communalism as a political arrangement that was neither theocratic nor communistic. A committed libertarian and a secularist, Fisher disagreed profoundly with those who saw early Mormon collectivism as a type of socialism.[24] Throughout *Children of God*, Brigham Young acts as a mouthpiece for Fisher's own political vision—one that avoids both the leveling impulse of socialism and the cruelty of *laissez-faire* capitalism: "He believed in personal initiative and competitive practice; but he also believed in collective community enterprises. He was aware of the wide range in human intelligence, talent, and ambition: there could never be a utopian society in which everyone could share equally; but there could be an order in which none needed to starve." Fisher ultimately concludes that what Brigham built was "the most remarkable social integration that had ever been achieved in the history of humankind."[25]

Together, Joseph Smith and Brigham Young create the dynamic and entirely original religious movement that Fisher documents in *Children of God*. From the former comes a new understanding of the human relationship to God and a bold challenge to nineteenth-century sexual norms. From the latter comes a radically new form of social organization that avoids the pitfalls of both unconstrained capitalism and hive-minded communism. When Joseph Flora claimed that Fisher "was clearly on the Mormon side in *Children of God*," he was almost certainly referring to the first two parts, which account for about 80 percent of the novel. In the final section, both the theological innovations of Joseph Smith and the social organization of Brigham Young slip away under pressure from the federal government for the Mormons to become just like everybody else.

The third part of *Children of God*, "Evening," shifts the point of view from Joseph Smith and Brigham Young to the fictional McBride family—Moroni, Tim, and Nephi—who had been minor characters in the first two parts of the book.[26] The three McBrides had been faithful followers of both Joseph Smith and Brigham Young, and they enthusiastically embraced Brigham's social vision to become the founding directors of Josephville, a United Order community modeled on the historical town of Orderville. When Brigham Young dies and his successor John Taylor goes into hiding, Nephi McBride warns that, if the Mormons "repudiate the principles God gave to Joseph, then our church will be only another church" and will become "no different than any other Protestant sect."[27]

"Evening" narrates the swift unraveling of Mormonism's unique world view. The catalyst for the unraveling is the federal government's anti-polygamy crusade, but the cause runs deeper. As Fisher constructs the narrative, both polygamy and the United Order require deep commitment and fundamental unselfishness that go beyond what most human beings can manage. The economic communalism of Josephville falls apart because people resent sharing with those people they see as less worthy. Polygamy falls apart for essentially the same reason. Petty squabbles and significant jealousy allow the larger society to impose its economic and sexual norms on one of the few societies that had managed to reject them.

The McBrides willingly endure the legal and judicial persecutions of the 1880s because they have accepted the vision. However, as the narrative progresses, they see everything they sacrificed for slipping away under the absent leadership of John Taylor and the assimilationist tendencies of the younger leaders. When Wilfred Woodruff issues the Manifesto ending plural marriage, Nephi McBride confronts him angrily, saying "go on and yield principle by principle until our church is only a wealthy corporation of special privilege and power! The covenant of plural marriage is gone. The Orders are destroyed. Those two were the blood and life of our religion."[28] Declaring that "the sun has set upon God's church," the McBrides leave Utah and go to Mexico, where they hope to be able to practice their religion in its fullness.[29] For Fisher, the Manifesto represented the end of Mormonism as a vital force and the beginning of a long assimilation that would turn it into another bland form of the American puritanism he despised.

Fisher's final judgment on Mormonism in the novel is that, after the death of Brigham Young, it ceased to be interesting. Five years after the publication of *Children of God*, Fisher wrote as much in a nonfiction essay for *Transatlantic* magazine. "Today Mormonism, after sixty years of battles and fifty years of healing its wounds, is merely another . . . of the Protestant sects," he wrote, echoing the words that he had earlier placed in the mouth of Nephi McBride. "It has had its prophet, its martyrdom and its ripening. Among the theologic tenets divulged by Joseph the offensive ones have been abandoned and the inoffensive ones have been kept."[30]

This final section of Fisher's novel had the greatest potential to alienate the Mormon hierarchy. Negative depictions of Joseph Smith's sexuality and Brigham Young's Machiavellianism were almost ridiculously commonplace in the 19th and early 20th centuries. One more novel about polygamous patriarchs and blood-atoning Danites would barely have registered with LDS leaders. But the charge that Mormonism lost its vitality after the 1890 Manifesto played directly into the hands of the Mormon fundamentalist movement that had recently become the LDS leadership's greatest problem.

Throughout the 1920s, Mormon fundamentalists—Latter-day Saints who rejected the Woodruff Manifesto and other accommodations that the Church made in the early 20th century—gathered strength among the many polygamists still alive; along with their children, they began to coalesce under the leadership of Lorin Woolley. Woolley, who had been a bodyguard and courier for high Church officials during the polygamy persecutions, claimed to possess the text of an 1886 revelation to President John Taylor commanding that the Church never abandon plural marriage. In 1934, Woolley and other polygamists formed "the Council of Friends" and, as historian Matthew Bowman writes, "immediately began to publish long theological tracts taking on the LDS church's claims to authority and refuting the validity of the Manifesto."[31] These theological tracts said many of the same things that the McBrides said at the end of *Children of God*. And a major writer's apparent endorsement of the fundamentalist argument could not have come at a worse moment for the Church.

Mormon Responses to *Children of God*

Scholarly consensus holds, quite incorrectly, that the Church of Jesus Christ of Latter-day Saints waged a public campaign against *Children of God*. This appears in the two most cited books about Fisher and his work published in the 20th century. In his 1965 critical study *Vardis Fisher*, Joseph M. Flora reports that "the Mormon church officially repudiated *Children of God*."[32] A generation later, in the only full-length biography of Fisher written to date, Boise journalist Tim Woodward wrote that "the Mormon Church repudiated it and for a time forbade its members to read it."[33] Both statements are, as far as the Utah-based Church of Jesus Christ of Latter-day Saints is concerned, completely false.

The one official Mormon statement about *Children of God* came from the Reorganized Church of Jesus Christ of Latter Day Saints (now the Community of Christ), with headquarters in Independence, Missouri, which published a review in the *Richmond Missourian* titled "*Children of God* by Vardis Fisher Is Not a Historical Novel." The statement read, in part, "it is an evil characterization of Joseph Smith and others who helped organize the Church and who lead it through early persecutions and hardships. Historical statements are distorted and woven into perverted situations in an obvious attempt to burlesque the Restoration movement."

The primary objection of the Reorganized Church, which developed from the Members of the Nauvoo Mormon Community who did not go West with Brigham Young, was that Fisher portrayed Joseph Smith as a polygamist. Church doctrine at the time held that Smith never practiced or sanctioned polygamy. "How can anyone," asks the official review, "believe that [Fisher] was honest in depicting scenes of depravity involving the sincerity and morals of Joseph Smith? The book panders to sensationalism and the sexual from beginning to end."[34]

The Utah Church was in a much more difficult position, as any response it made had to address both non-Mormons—who might be negatively influenced by portrayals of Joseph Smith and Brigham Young and the practice of polygamy—and its own membership, who might be tempted to agree with Fisher that plural marriage was a vital doctrine that had been abandoned without God's sanction. The logical person to make the response was Elder John A. Widtsoe. One of the first Latter-day Saint Apostles to hold a PhD, Widtsoe had been president of the University of Utah during the time that Vardis Fisher was a student. Widtsoe was the editor of the Church's official magazine, the *Improvement Era*, for which he wrote a monthly feature called "On the Book Rack" containing short capsule reviews of books that might interest Latter-day Saints.

In August of 1939, Widtsoe wrote a review of *Children of God* for the *Improvement Era*. The review was harsh, but not without praise for the author's technical skill. And it focused on what Widtsoe and others saw as Fisher's unfair portrayal of both Joseph Smith and Brigham Young. The review ran to three paragraphs—much longer than the normal one-paragraph reviews that Widtsoe wrote—and sharply criticized Fisher's portrayals of the Mormon prophets. In Fisher's novel, he wrote,

> we are asked to believe that spiritual power and great material conquests come out of filthy, coarse, and unlovely lives. To one familiar with Mormon literature the book is but another addition to the heap of inaccurate or biased or malicious writings about Mormonism. To the stranger it can be only the story of a pitifully deluded people, led first by a dreaming dishonest sex pervert, then by a profane, tyrannical murderer, followed by two weaklings, one stubborn, the other a coward—with salacious stories and suggestions holding the events together.[35]

Widtsoe knew that a review by a senior apostle in a Church publication would have been seen as an official response by the Church, so he sent the review to his coeditor, Richard L. Evans, with a note that "the review should no doubt be considered by the First Presidency." He added that "they may decide that silence is the better part of wisdom," but that "the importance of the book makes silence seem of doubtful value."[36] The First Presidency at the time—consisting of Heber J. Grant, J. Rueben Clark, and David O. McKay—did decide on silence, and neither the *Improvement Era* nor any other official LDS forum acknowledged the publication or existence of *Children of God*. When Church members wrote to inquire about the Church's position on Fisher or the book, Widtsoe responded that "we paid no attention to the book itself in our Church publications."[37]

Widtsoe did occasionally send out copies of his review to others, though, and it played an important role in the Church's behind-the-scenes efforts to prevent *Children of God* from influencing Twentieth Century Fox's 1940 epic film *Brigham Young*. Fox producer Darryl Zanuck had purchased the film rights several months before its publication, leading Fisher to hope— and LDS authorities to fear—that the novel would become the basis for a major motion picture that would introduce Mormon history to millions of people. Both the hope and the fear were misplaced. By the time that Fox executives heard about Fisher's novel, they had already authorized the Brigham Young movie, developed the storyline, and commissioned a well-known novelist to write the script.

However, the well-known novelist that Fox hired to write the script was Louis Bromfield, one of the three judges who awarded the Harper Prize to Vardis Fisher. After reading the novel in manuscript version, Bromfield convinced Zanuck to purchase the film rights from Fisher to prevent the possibility of a lawsuit.[38] Though Fisher was offended that his novel was being purchased for "nuisance value," he sold the rights for $4,400.[39] When this news reached LDS Church headquarters, Widtsoe sent a copy of his unpublished review, along with a letter offering his assistance as a technical advisor, to Kenneth Macgowan, the studio executive in charge of the production.[40] Macgowan responded by quoting a passage that he had written to Heber J. Grant a few weeks earlier, after Fox executives visiting Salt Lake City reported the First Presidency's extreme displeasure with Fisher's novel:

> We felt that from it we could get some aid in approximating the type of dialogue and popular expression of the time but, apart from this, I believe we shall have to rely on our own writers and the considerable mass of research which you and the writers of the past have been able to give us. We felt that it was the best policy to buy this book since it had inadvertently been read by Mr. Bromfield before reporting to work and we should have found ourselves in an awkward situation if the writer had seen fit to go to court with any claims of plagiarism, however ill founded.[41]

Grant asked Widtsoe to serve as the Church's liaison to Fox for the duration of the film project, and Macgowan gave him the opportunity to read and critique various drafts of the script.[42] Fisher, on the other hand, was never consulted. In fact, because the marketing plan for the film required a huge opening in Utah, Macgowan took active steps to eliminate anything in the film that could even suggest *Children of God* as a source. In an internal memo dated April 30, 1940, he wrote to studio publicist Harry Brand letting him know that he had asked scriptwriters to rework a scene that still had some of Fisher's dialogue in it and go through and compare the screenplay and the novel so that they knew "exactly what dialogue to avoid."[43] Though the final film *Brigham Young-Frontiersman* covered some of the same historical events and figures as Vardis Fisher did, it contained nothing that could have tied it to *Children of God*.

Children of God and the Golden Age of Mormon Literature

Within three years of the publication of *Children of God*, eight more Mormon-themed novels were published by national presses, including Houghton Mifflin, Bobbs-Merrill, Alfred A. Knopf, and Macmillan.[44] Fisher's novel opened up a space in the market for books that fell between the scandalous adventure stories of the Mormon frontier and the faith-promoting stories published by the Church.[45] Four of these eight books were written by current or former Latter-day Saints who presented Mormonism as the source of compelling and deeply human stories. These books, along with *Children of God* itself, constitute the nucleus of what would eventually become the basis of the academic study of Mormon literature.

The first two novels to appear after *Children of God*—Jean Maw Woodman's *Glory Spent* and Paul Bailey's *For This My Glory*—were well underway when Fisher won the Harper Prize in June of 1939. Woodman grew up in Provo, where her father was chair of the BYU Chemistry Department for many years. When Fisher's novel first appeared, she had been working for some time on her novel *Glory Spent*—the story of three generations of a Mormon family living in Provo and the changing ways that the women of each generation understood their relationship to the Church. The youngest heroine, like Woodman, eventually leaves the Church and Utah for adventures in the non-Mormon world.

Woodman began the novel at the suggestion of her friend Lynn Carrick, who had just left the editorial staff of Lippincott to start his own imprint called Carrick & Evans. Carrick believed, and told Woodman, that the Mormon experience was a wholly unique subject for contemporary fiction.[46] News of the Harper Prize award to *Children of God* originally devastated Woodman. After a discouraging phone call, Carrick, who feared that she might not finish the book, wrote to assure her that Fisher's book would not interfere with her book in the marketplace. "I'm afraid I may have over-emphasized to you the novel aspects of the background when we first talked," he acknowledged. "Our interest is in no way lessened, and certainly as good a book as yours promises to be should not be seriously affected." He also sounded a note of encouragement: "I have no doubt that *Children of God* will prove a best seller, since all indications are that it is an excellent book, but the interest it stirs up may even prove a help when your novel comes along."[47]

Glory Spent was published in March of 1940 with enthusiastic reviews. It was almost immediately grouped with *Children of God* by reviewers, who noted that Fisher narrated "the stirring history of Mormonism" while Woodman described "the present-day members of the colony."[48] Several literary heavy hitters weighed in. Stephen Vincent Benet wrote a glowing review in the *New York Herald Tribune*.[49] And Phyllis McGinley praised it as "the first book to give "an actual picture of Mormonism and one that "makes Mormonism credible and the Saints the ordinary Americans which they are."[50] And perhaps the most effusive review of all came in the Provo *Daily Herald* and was written by Frank C. Robertson, whose 1936 Mormon novel *The Rocky Road to Jericho* was all but ignored in his home state. He introduced *Glory Spent* as "what should be to Utah readers, at least, the most significant novel of the year."[51]

The connection between *Glory Spent* and *Children of God* became even clearer when Fisher himself agreed to review Woodman's novel for the *Saturday Review*. Ironically, Fisher's review was one of the few negative reviews that the book received. Even more ironically, his main complaint was that Woodman treated the Mormon characters too harshly: "It is not clear to me, for instance, what purpose is served in making the father a bungling dreamer," he complained. "No doubt there are such Mormons in small Utah and Idaho towns, but the hard-headed, thrifty, money-grubbing realists are a more common and relevant type." Similarly, Fisher felt that the female main character's Mormon boyfriend was portrayed with "a little more obtuseness sand smugness than was necessary." For Fisher, the result of these characterizations was a novel that unfairly blames the Mormon religion for what are really the problems that talented young women experience in small towns everywhere. "Such spirited girls," he concludes, "also run away from small towns in Iowa or New York."[52]

A few months later, in October of 1940, a young Mormon writer named Paul Bailey published *For This My Glory* with the Los Angeles firm Lyman House. Bailey's book covered almost the same historical events and characters as Fisher's, but *For This My Glory* presented a much more favorable picture of the Saints. The publication of Bailey's book was partially orchestrated by John A. Widtsoe, who saw in the book, and in Bailey, a chance to use the Church's influence and purchasing power to sponsor its own rebuttal to *Children of God*. Bailey sent a draft of the book to Widtsoe in 1939 with the title *Hell's Serenade*. Widtsoe read and liked the manuscript and corresponded frequently with the author, who shopped the novel around to New York publishers for more than a year and received multiple rejections.

Widtsoe and Bailey exchanged more than 60 letters with each other between 1939 and 1944. With Widtsoe's encouragement, Bailey revised the novel several times, each time making it friendlier to the Church. "The more I think of Mormon exploitation of the book," he wrote to his agent, "the more certain I feel that the market here to be plucked should be good for enough books to underwrite the financial hazards of publishing the book, and leave national sales as gravy."[53] With Widtsoe's help—including assurances that the Church would purchase a substantial number of copies and sell them in its bookstores—Bailey secured a contract. A year later, Widtsoe arranged for Bailey's novel to become part of the Mutual Improvement Association curriculum, which turned it into a regional best seller, eventually selling 28,000 copies—an almost unheard-of accomplishment for a book from a small press marketed only to Latter-day Saints.[54]

Bailey went on to write several other Mormon-themed novels that were less friendly to the Church. His final novel, *For Time and All Eternity* (1964), which explored the polygamy persecutions of the 1880s, became a national best seller and was given the same silent treatment by the Church that *Children of God* was given 25 years earlier. But he continued to acknowledge that his breakthrough with *For This My Glory* was possible because the Mormons needed "an antidote to their people for the stinging venom of Fisher's Children of God."[55]

The next pair of Mormon novels to follow Fisher into print, Maurine Whipple's *The Giant Joshua* (1941) and Virginia Sorensen's *A Little Lower than the Angels* (1942), would end up having a greater impact on the development of Mormon literature than anything that came before them—including *Children of God*. Both books focused on smaller stories that fell within Fisher's epic sweep. *The Giant Joshua* takes place between 1861 and 1884, during the mission to colonize St. George. *A Little Lower than the Angels* is contained entirely within the Nauvoo period of Mormon history, from 1839 through 1846. Both authors also created strong female heroines based on their own ancestors. The protagonist of *The Giant Joshua*, Clorinda Agatha "Clory" McIntyre, is based on Whipple's own maternal grandmother, Cornelia Agatha McAllister.[56] And Mercy Baker, the young Mormon wife through whose eyes Sorensen narrates the rise and fall of Nauvoo, was her husband's great-grandmother. In true Mormon fashion, both of these writers used their novels as a way to explore their family histories.

The action of *The Giant Joshua* fits neatly into the third part of *Children of God*. It covers the same time period as the McBride family's story and invokes many of the same themes: the settling of new territory, the creation of a communal order based on Joseph Smith's idea of Zion, and the impact of the 1890 Manifesto ending plural marriage on the lives and the faith of ordinary Latter-day Saints. The two novels, however, approach their subject matter very differently. *Children of God* is a novel of ideas. Fisher was fascinated with the communitarian impulses behind both polygamy and the United Order, and he saw the abandonment of these ideas as the end of any genuine vitality in Mormonism. For Fisher, it is the power of big ideas that give significance to the actions of the characters, who function primarily as allegorical representations of the ideas that they represent.

The Giant Joshua, on the other hand, is concerned with the lived experience of its characters. The novel revolves around the life of Clory MacIntyre from her plural marriage at 16 to the man who raised her as a father, through her experiences with the small colony that Brigham Young sent to St. George to start a cotton industry, all the way through the anti-polygamy persecutions of the 1880s. Both polygamy and economic communalism contribute to the parade of brutality that Clory experiences in St. George: poverty, humiliation, famine, plague, the deaths of her children, and the final betrayal of her husband. Whipple does not share Fisher's reverence for polygamy and the United Order; these are much smaller ideas in *The Giant Joshua* than they are in *Children of God*. The bigger idea in Whipple's narrative is expressed by Apostle Erastus Snow, the historical figure who led the mission to St. George. "I believe it to be Zion's mission to mankind," Snow tells Clory, "to create among these barren hills a little inviolate world

. . . where the Brotherhood of Man and the Fatherhood of God are not just words but living, breathing realities."[57]

But even Apostle Snow's grand vision is too abstract to capture the significance of Clory's experience. Talking about big ideas is the prerogative of the male characters in *The Giant Joshua*. Clory, her sister wives, and the other female characters are wholly invested in bearing children, creating homes, finding food, and keeping their families alive—things that they do out of necessity to manage the consequences of choices that they did not make. The religious ideas in the novel are important as a consequence of Clory's actions, not as their cause. Through suffering and sacrifice, Clory and the other women in the novel consecrate the underlying religious ideas and endow them with a sacredness, and a significance, that they would otherwise lack. And at the end of the novel, Clory, on her death bed, determines that her life, while not easy, has been meaningful.

Whipple's novel is much messier than Fisher's. Its plot is less focused, and at times it reads more like a collection of short vignettes with the same settings and characters. But its account of both polygamy and religious community rang truer to the descendants of the pioneers than Fisher's account did, and it has therefore enjoyed more recognition within Mormon culture as an important literary work. Terryl Givens concludes that its focus on the dramatic tensions of Mormon identity make it "perhaps the fullest cultural expression of the Mormon experience." And Eugene England, who worked hard to resurrect interest in Whipple's work throughout his career, called *The Giant Joshua* "the richest, fullest, most moving, the *truest* fiction about the Great Basin pioneer experience that I have found."[58]

Like *The Giant Joshua*, Virginia Sorensen's *A Little Lower than the Angels* takes a small portion of the history contained in *Children of God* and uses it as the basis for a more contained and more domestic drama. Historically, Sorensen's novel takes place during Mormonism's Nauvoo period (1839–1845). Like Fisher, Sorensen uses Joseph Smith as a main character whose actions drive much of the plot; however, he is not a viewpoint character. His words and actions are filtered through the eyes of Mercy Baker, a non-Mormon woman who comes to Nauvoo with her recently converted husband, Simon, and their five children. As the novel progresses, Mercy is baptized, though she never really becomes a believer, and she bears four more children—all the while serving as a witness to the rise and fall of Nauvoo.

Sorensen grants Mercy extraordinary access to the lives of important figures. She is among the first citizens of Nauvoo to meet John C. Bennett when he becomes the new mayor, and she forms a close friendship with Eliza R. Snow—so close that, when Joseph Smith takes Eliza as his plural wife, Mercy is the only woman invited to witness the ceremony. She immediately understands how insidious and how consequential Joseph's new doctrine will be. She understands that it will soon become part of the Church and that it will tempt her own husband and threaten to destroy their family.[59] She then watches helplessly as the doctrine of plural marriage spreads through Nauvoo, causing jealousy and dissension that eventually congeals into the mob that takes Joseph Smith's life. And she endures the betrayal that she has long feared when, soon after Joseph's death, Brigham Young convinces Simon to take another wife.

Like Whipple, Sorensen counters Fisher's intellectual appreciation of early Mormonism's most distinctive doctrines—polygamy and communitarianism—with the lived experience of a woman who is compelled to be a part of it. Unlike Clory MacIntyre, however, Mercy Baker lives in the center of the novel's Mormon world. She watches as the doctrine of polygamy develops, but she watches helplessly, aware of what is happening and unable to prevent it. Nor does she ever find the meaning or validation that Clory finds at the end of her life. Despite her proximity to the key figures in Mormon history, and her life of sacrifice for the principles that they articulated, she never becomes a believer, which makes *A Little Lower than the Angels* a more forceful critique of Mormon history than either *Children of God* or *The Giant Joshua*.

Like both Vardis Fisher and Maurine Whipple, Virginia Sorensen attracted partisans who viewed her novel as the greatest literary use of the Mormon story to date. One such partisan was Wallace Stegner, Fisher's former student, who wrote in the *Saturday Review* that

> If writers are miners and history ore, it was inevitable that Mormonism would sooner or later be exploited and shipped off to the literary stamp mills, even if Bernard DeVoto hadn't tempted Providence three years ago by guessing that the Mormon story was too big to handle. Nobody up to now has proved Mr. DeVoto wrong. Virginia Sorensen, in this admirable first novel, comes very close to doing just that. Instead of trying to cover the whole panorama of Mormon history . . . she confines herself to the history of Nauvoo.[60]

Stegner did not mention Fisher by name, because he didn't have to. Anyone reading *Saturday Review* in 1942 would have known who tried "to cover the whole panorama of Mormon history." And most readers would have understood that, in saying that "nobody up to now has proved Mr. DeVoto wrong," Stegner was pronouncing *Children of God* a failure—or, at least, an inferior book when compared to *A Little Lower than the Angels*. Alfred Knopf himself said the same thing, though much more clearly. "I think your novel so much better that the two simply cannot be mentioned in the same breath," he wrote her when *Angels* was published. "I think Fisher's a very pedestrian, unexciting performance which must have sold solely because of its sheer, overwhelming bulk."[61]

With the publication of *A Little Lower than the Angels*, it became clear that *Children of God* was not an isolated novel about Mormon history, but the start of a genuine movement in regional literature that took both Mormon history and Mormon culture seriously as the subject of fiction. By 1942, the eminent Utah historian Dale Morgan felt confident saying that Fisher's novel had been the start of something new and vital in Mormon letters: "In the autumn of 1942," he wrote, "we can number nine novels that have proceeded from the presses since *Children of God*, in 1939, ushered in the new dispensation. These nine novels represent the individual responses of an astonishing variety of authors to an anomalous literary vacuum and will have their weight in all further writing on the Mormon theme."[62]

Morgan was right. At least a dozen more Mormon novels were published between 1943 and 1949, three more novels by Paul Bailey and two by Virginia Sorensen.[63] This list included two novels whose popularity far eclipsed *Children of God* in popularity: Samuel Taylor's comic novel *Heaven Knows Why* (1948), which was first serialized to more than 5 million readers in *Collier's Magazine* under the title *The Mysterious Way*; and Ardyth Kennelly's *The Peaceable Kingdom* (1949), which as a main selection of the Literary Guild sold nearly a half a million copies.[64]

Years later, when Mormon literary scholars began the historical work of canon-building, the remarkable period of regional writing between 1939 and 1949 became known as "the Lost Generation"—an allusion to the expatriate American writers of the 1920s.[65] This term makes sense only when seen from the perspective of rigid orthodoxy and loyalty to the Church of Jesus Christ of Latter-day Saints—a perspective that is inherently at odds with the sort of nationally prominent literature that literary scholars study. However lost their generation may have been, though, the principle figures of this movement—Fisher, Bailey, Whipple, Sorensen, and Taylor—quickly became the backbone of the nascent discipline of Mormon Literature, whose attempts to reclaim Vardis Fisher as a part of its tradition met with the scorn and legal threats of Fisher's widow. And yet, it would be impossible to discuss, or even to begin to analyze the outpouring of Mormon-themed regional literature that occurred in the 1940s without recognizing the role that Vardis Fisher and *Children of God* played in setting that movement in motion and creating both the critical environment and the literary market that allowed so many remarkable works to flourish.

CHAPTER FOUR

The Not Quite
Not Mormon Worldview
of the *Testament of Man*

Some boys were introverted by the scornful tyrannies of
women and driven to seek precious values of their own.
The prophet has always been one who, striving first to
justify his existence and impelled by his hunger to look
beyond accepted customs, discovers that he has evolved a
philosophy. He has to convince himself as well as others,
and the faith of others promotes his own faith in himself.

—Vardis Fisher, *Adam and the Serpent*, Book 4 of the
Testament of Man

In 1943, Vardis Fisher had written ten novels and was one of only a handful
of American writers rumored to be "important." He had achieved critical
acclaim (and modest financial success) in three different areas: his early
novels about the Snake River region of Idaho had been praised as examples
of Western regional fiction and compared favorably to John Steinbeck and
William Faulkner. The four autobiographical novels of his *Tetralogy* were
grouped, with the works of his friend Thomas Wolfe, as premier examples
of the confessional novel. And his epic novel of the Mormon migration,
Children of God, had recently won one of the most important literary prizes
in the country and had established Fisher as a major historical novelist.
Had he focused on any combination of these three areas, he would have
had a very different—and almost certainly a more lucrative—writing career.

But Fisher did not want to be known primarily as a Western writer, or as
an Idaho writer—and he certainly did not want to be known as a Mormon
writer. He had bigger dreams to chase. In 1943, he published *Darkness and
the Deep*, the first novel in the *Testament of Man*—a twelve-book epic cycle

that would consume most of his time and considerable talent for the next twenty years. The project was the historical novel conceived on a grand scale. He set out to tell nothing less than the religious, psychological, social, and sexual history of humanity.

It was a big job, and, though some of the initial novels sold well, the series itself did so poorly, and caused such controversy, that Fisher had great difficulty finding publishers for most of the later novels in the series. As Fisher's biographer Tim Woodward writes, the *Testament of Man* series "would cost him twenty of his most productive years, a close friend and publisher, and any hope of maintaining the reputation he briefly enjoyed as one of the nation's up-and-coming novelists." However, as Woodward understands, "he wasn't writing the *Testament* for the best-seller lists. He was convinced he was writing it for the ages."[1]

Unfortunately, the ages have been no kinder to the *Testament of Man* than its initial readers and critics were. All twelve books have been out of print for decades—and most of them are difficult to find even in libraries and used bookstores. Though the series did provide the subject matter for a few MA theses and PhD dissertations in the 1970s, there has been very little scholarly work on the *Testament* since then.[2] In one of the few recent treatments of the *Testament*, written for a centennial celebration of Fisher's work edited by Joseph Flora and published by the University of Idaho Press, anthropologist Marilyn Trent Grunkmeyer calls the series "a massive exposition of one of the greatest perduring male fantasies of all time" and refers to its capstone final volume as "spiritually exhausting and emotionally toxic."[3] The further we get from Fisher's source material, and the time-bound anthropological assumptions that inform Fisher's work, the less likely it becomes that the *Testament of Man* will ever experience a massive resurgence in either popular or scholarly interest.

But there is much in the *Testament of Man* worth appreciating. For one thing, most of the novels are pretty good. Fisher was a novelist of ideas, but, unlike most novelists of ideas, he also knew how to tell a compelling story. And in the second decade of the 21st century, *Testament of Man* provides fascinating glimpses into the state of anthropology and religious studies halfway through the 20th century. In preparing to write these novels, Fisher read thousands of works written from the 1890s through the 1960s, and what he incorporates in the novel represents a pretty good sampling of the state of anthropological scholarship during his lifetime.[4] If it is a failure, it is a noble one—and therefore worth studying as one of the 20th century's great cautionary tales: the one about the gifted writer whose reach exceeded his grasp.

And though the *Testament of Man* does not contain a Mormon-themed book other than *Orphans in Gethsemane*, in which Fisher rewrites and expands the autobiographical tetralogy, the plan of the series required Fisher to grapple with all of the received opinions of the society that shaped him—including the Mormon ones. The twelve official volumes in the series treated topics that had much to do with Vridar's (and therefore Vardis's) upbringing—things like religion, sexuality, rationality, prophecy, and guilt. These are not inherently Mormon themes, but they are all themes about which Mormonism has much to say. If Fisher really did use these novels to try to understand the ideas and prejudices that formed his younger self, then we should expect to see traces of a recognizably Mormon worldview mixed in with everything else—a bread-crumb trail leading back to the religion of his youth.

And we do. The characterizations of Mormonism lie beneath the surface of the books in the *Testament of Man* series, but they are not buried deep underground. Fisher's only personal exposure to religion came through his Mormon faith. And Vridar Hunter—the common antitype of every protagonist in the series—spent the first decades of his life as a Mormon. When Fisher writes about prophets, religious community, or sexual guilt, he filters his words through both the scholarship that he read and the experiences that he had. And many of those experiences, as we have already seen, were fundamentally Mormon.

Another Testament

Fisher's plan in the *Testament of Man* series—creating a third "testament" to expand on and correct the other two—has a distinctly Mormon flavor. It is structurally, if not ideologically, the plan of the Book of Mormon, which also bills itself as "another testament."[5] Fisher's testament, of course, is primarily secular and scholarly. But it shares a common narrative arc with the Book of Mormon. Both encompass the time periods of the Old and New Testaments of the Christian Bible; both contain multiple type scenes that connect it to biblical events such as the Fall and the Exodus;[6] and both bring Jesus Christ on the stage about 2/3 of the way through to effect a fundamental chance in the social order.

The scriptural aspects of the *Testament* go well beyond its name. Though Fisher accepts neither the theology nor the history of the Bible, he borrows extensively from its structure in ways that are, if not explicitly Mormon, at least unmistakably Christian. The borrowing begins with the long chapter on the creation of the world in *Darkness and the Deep*. While Fisher clearly sees himself as a good Darwinist and wants to explain the "creation" of the world in evolutionary terms, we can catch glimpses from the very beginning of an implied author who is not quite as irreligious as he wants us to believe. Consider the following passage from the "creation" story:

> These single-celled invisible organisms multiplied into many cells and grew into colonies, and the colonies in time became masses of seaweed. . . . But stored in them was an urge, sleepless, constant, and working in its own sorcerous way, toward a life more various and abundant and self-determined. There was an urge to sink roots, to become more than the buffeted flotsam of the sea. There was, indeed, in this simple primitive urge, this feeling, this inheritance from time and darkness, the will toward legs that would walk and wings that would fly; because everything that was to be upon this earth was stored there in the algae drifting by the ocean's shores.[7]

No Christian would ever mistake this passage for a biblical account of creation, of course, but neither could any true Darwinist mistake it for a valid evolutionary narrative. It implies precisely the teleological view of evolution that principled Darwinism must reject—the view that evolution somehow began with the end in mind, or that the current configuration of life, including sentient human beings, has always been implied in the evolutionary narrative.

Some critics have characterized this and other similar passages in *Darkness and the Deep* (1943) as "Lamarckian," or based on Jean Baptist-Lamarck's pre-Darwinian theory "that acquired characteristics could be biologically inherited."[8] For several reasons, though, the charge of Lamarckianism fails to explain the opening chapter of *Darkness and the Deep*. In the first place, Fisher read widely before writing the *Testament*, and he knew perfectly well that Darwinian natural selection had much earlier displaced Lamarckian inherited change as the dominant paradigm for evolution. More importantly, though, Lamarckian evolution is no more inherently teleological than natural selection. Fisher's claim that evolution began in a way that led inexorably to creatures like us is neither Darwinian nor

Lamarckian; it is theological. It requires (even as it pretends to deny) the presence of a cosmic intelligence directing the evolutionary process to a predetermined end. And this is precisely the kind of conceptual error that we might expect from someone who has intellectually rejected religion and everything associated with it but who continues to harbor affinities for something that looks an awful lot like God.

The remainder of *Darkness and the Deep* narrates the experience of a group of *Australopithecus* hominids—early human ancestors who lived between two and four million years ago. The follow-up novel, *The Golden Rooms* (1944) splits its perspective between Neanderthal and Cro-Magnon tribes, ending with a local massacre of the former by the latter that readers understand to represent the genocide that some scholars believe to have occurred some 35,000 years ago. This act of evolutionary fratricide invokes, even as it naturalizes, the story of Cain and Abel.[9] The next two novels— *Imitations of Eve* (1946) and *Adam and the Serpent* (1947)—explore the now-debunked hypothesis that early human society was matriarchal and became patriarchal only by the introduction of the monotheistic worship of the sun. The people of this novel become the world's first monotheists and the ancestors of the Hebrews in the Bible.[10]

The first four *Testament of Man* novels offer a highly naturalistic, de-mythologized rewriting of the Book of Genesis, and, like Genesis, they describe the history of the world through the creation to the introduction of a recognizably Hebraic religion. The next novel, *The Divine Passion* (1948), continues the biblical structure by telling, in a similarly naturalistic way, the story of the Exodus. This is not the dramatic escape from slavery in Egypt narrated in the Bible, however; rather, it is the story of how one village led by an arrogant despot and a fanatical prophet tries to conquer a nearby village—a "land flowing with milk and honey"—and fails. Convinced that their defeat was caused by lust for women, the prophet Yescha tries to castrate himself and fails, producing the ritual of circumcision. When Yescha dies, the people dedicate themselves to his religion and—presumably, for the novel ends soon after the prophet's death—succeeded and become the Nation of Israel. This novel includes naturalistic versions of many other Exodus-inspired tropes, such as God speaking from a burning bush, atonement sacrifices, a divine covenant, initial versions of some of the Ten Commandments, and an insistence on a specific tribe as "a chosen people."[11]

The rest of the novels in *The Testament of Man* all deal with periods and events that are part of recorded history. Two of these are recognizably Old

Testament or Intertestamental: the reign of Solomon (*The Valley of Vision*, 1951) and the Maccabean rebellion (*The Island of the Innocent*, 1952) and the rest come from the New Testament or the Christian tradition: the life of Jesus (*Jesus Came Again*, 1956), the early Christian movements (*A Goat for Azazel*, 1956), the World of the Desert Fathers (*Peace Like a River*, 1957), and the Inquisition (*My Holy Satan*, 1958). The final novel in the series, the nearly 1,000-page *Orphans in Gethsemane* (1960), is a revision and updating of the *Tetralogy* novels in which Fisher tells his own story through the eyes of his fictional alter ego, Vridar Hunter.

But really, all twelve books are autobiographical. Each of the first 11 novels has at least one character who is a recognizable type of Vridar Hunter in *Orphans in Gethsemane*. Scholars have long recognized the typological nature of the series. "The research behind his books is tremendous," writes Fisher scholar Joseph M. Flora, but the primary strategy of the Testament is "to imagine what Vridar would have done in the times Fisher considers." Tim Woodward explains the *Testament of Man* series as "an attempt to rewrite the Vridar story in a way that sheds light not just on Vridar, but on all the Vridars—the confused, frightened neurotics whom he presently came to call orphans." And this way of telling a story is also biblical.

This typological association of a figure from one book with a character still to come is yet another structural device that Fisher borrows from the Bible—or at least the Bible as Christians read it. Christian figural interpretation has long held that many of the main characters in the Old Testament—Abraham, Moses, David, Jonah, and so on—were types of the Christ to come—and that Jesus Christ, therefore, is the antitype of the heroes of the Old Testament. Their lives, characteristics, and major accomplishments predicted Christ in some major way: Moses led the Children of Israel out of Egypt in the same way that Christ would lead the souls of believers out of sin; Jonah stayed three days in the whale's belly as Christ would stay three days in the tomb—and so on. This is the reason that Christians call the Hebrew Bible a "testament" of Jesus Christ. And in the same way that the heroes of the Bible point typologically to the great hero to come, the various protagonists of the *Testament of Man* all point typologically to Vridar Hunter.

The Vridar character in each novel is usually a brilliant social misfit with profound creative energy, equally profound neurosis, and deep doubts about the society that he lives in. In the first two novels, the Vridar characters—the *Australopithecus* Wuh, the Neanderthal Harg, and the Cro-Magnon Gode—do well for themselves. They analyze things more carefully than their peers and, as a result, devise strategies that give them great social prominence and mating opportunities. As the societies of the *Testament* become matriarchal, though, the Vridar characters start to lose power. And as the matriarchal religion becomes more prominent, the Vridar Hunter types in the novels are pushed further and further out to the margins—until they rebel against the matriarchy and replace it with a monotheistic patriarchy with no place for the divine feminine.

In the third book of the Testament, *Intimations of Eve*, Fisher gives us some intriguing clues about the autobiographical nature of the entire *Testament*. The Vridar-type in this novel is a man named Raven who suffers as a marginal male figure in a wholly matriarchal culture. The one responsibility that men have in this culture is to hunt and provide food for their families. The women of the tribe hold Raven in contempt because he lacks skill as a hunter. About halfway through the book, however, he turns his fortunes around by inventing fishing:

> Lying on his belly, with his feet thrust across to keep the canoe balanced, he would look over the edge and poise his lance. Then he would slowly lower the lance into the water and wait for a fish to swim under the point; whereupon, with a short swift jab, he would impale it.
>
> He toiled earnestly, spearing one after another and interrupting his labor to take each to the bank, lest he tip over and spill his cargo; and when at last he went home, walking like one who had breached the last barriers between his family and starvation, he took about thirty pounds of fish.[12]

The linguistic symbolism here could not be clearer: the "Hunter" saves himself and his family by becoming the "Fisher." Vridar becomes Vardis, thus parting the veil between the author and his alter ego.

The significance of this symbolic self-identification continues through most of the middle books of the *Testament*. Along with being a bad hunter and a good fisher, Raven is also the first character in the novels that we can consider a "prophet"—or a figure who discovers and announces religious principles. The specific principle that Raven discovers is "a sense of good and evil, of human responsibility, and of benevolent and malign beings; and the vague idea of human responsibility was leading him in turn to a sense of sin." By "inventing" sin, Raven changes the trajectory of the entire human race, as his invention will be seized upon by other prophets and incorporated into the religions that they create. In the next novel, *Adam and the Serpent*, Fisher introduces the counterpart to Raven, a man named "Dove" who is explicitly labeled a prophet. "The prophet," he writes, "has always been one who, striving first to justify his existence and impelled by his hunger to look beyond accepted customs, discovers that he has evolved a philosophy. He has to convince himself as well as others, and the faith of others promotes his own faith in himself."[13]

This passage should leap to the attention of anyone looking for a vestigial Mormon worldview in the *Testament of Man*. Prophets do not presume Mormonism, of course, as they are found throughout the Old Testament. But no Old Testament prophet even comes close to fitting the definition that Fisher offers here: a somewhat insecure boy who feels compelled to search for truth, look beyond accepted customs, evolve a philosophy, and influence others to accept it. Nothing in the Old Testament suggests that Samuel or Nathan ever had to strive to justify their own existence, or that Isaiah or Ezekiel were "impelled by their hunger to look beyond accepted customs." The prophets of the Old Testament were religious conservatives. They called people to repentance and warned them of impending doom— but they always did so in the name of the established religion. The prophet that Fisher describes in *Adam and the Serpent*—who evolves and announces spectacular new religious truths—is a religious radical.

The one prophet-figure who fits Fisher's description in nearly every detail is Joseph Smith—if not the historical one at least the version of Joseph Smith that Fisher created for *Children of God*. As Fisher presents him, Joseph Smith is a good-natured, inquisitive young man who constantly reasons his way to religious "truths" that he announces to his followers in the name of God. He has an expansive but untrained mind that constantly looks beyond accepted customs—whether they are religious, cultural, or social. And he, much more than Ezekiel or Isaiah, is the logical heir of prophets such as Raven and Dove in *Testament of Man*. Fisher acknowledges as much in the first section of *Orphans in Gethsemane*, the revised version of the autobiographical tetralogy that becomes the final novel in the *Testament of Man*. As a very young boy, Vridar Hunter announces to his mother that he wants to grow up to be a prophet, and immediately she invokes the only prophet she knows anything about. "She encouraged him," Fisher writes, "She said that in the last hundreds of years there had been only one prophet, Joseph Smith, who founded a church in which alone there was truth."[14]

Like Vridar Hunter, Vardis Fisher had a strong-willed mother who influenced him well into his adulthood. She was one of the two Mormon women who influenced almost every aspect of his life. The other was his first wife, the former Leona McMurtrey, whom he courted and married when he still identified as a Mormon. Dealing with the Mormon views of those closest to him becomes one of Vridar's most difficult challenges in *Orphans in Gethsemane*. And this, in turn, becomes one of the most important recurring motifs in the *Testament*: the religious nonbeliever who interacts obsessively with a religion and its culture as a way to better understand an important woman in his life.

This motif becomes the central theme of at least two of the later novels: *The Island of the Innocent* (Book 7), in which an educated Greek doctor falls in love with a beautiful Jewish woman and joins the Maccabean rebellion on the side of the Jews; and *A Goat for Azazel* (Book 9), in which a young Roman intellectual travels throughout the empire trying to understand Christianity after seeing his Christian mother willingly accept martyrdom for her faith. Both characters end up influencing, and being strongly influenced by, religious cultures whose religions they do not accept.

Island of the Innocent: Faith as an Intellectual Exercise

The seventh novel of the *Testament of Man*, *The Island of the Innocent*, takes place in Jerusalem before and during the Maccabean Revolt, which began in 167 BCE and is treated in the deuterocanonical books of First and Second Maccabees. In his retrospective overview of the *Testament*, Fisher describes this as a pivotal moment for all of the major themes that he treats. "The extremely bitter struggle between Jews who wanted to Hellenize Israel and those who wanted to preserve it in racial and religious isolation—the struggle between beauty and righteousness—was of transcendent importance," he notes. "Allergic to women and to practically all pleasures, the lean, shaggy, angry prophets won a second time. The price the . . . Vridars paid for that victory no one, so far as I know, has ever tried to determine."[15]

The two worldviews that Fisher alludes to here—"beauty and righteousness," or, to use the especially apt Arnoldian terms, "Hellenism" and "Hebraism,"—conflict constantly throughout *Testament of Man*.[16] The two novels preceding *Island of the Innocent* represent the conflict allegorically, with paired characters who each represent one end of the dichotomy. In *The Divine Passion*, the priest named Rabi, represents the Hellenistic impulse. He is artistically and intellectually curious, socially liberal, and anxious to accommodate human nature. The opposite view, the Hebraic impulse, comes in the form of Yescha, the self-declared prophet, who believes that women are the source of evil, that sex is inherently sinful, and that humanity can be saved only by rigid adherence to an uncompromising law. In *The Valley of Vision*, King Solomon represents the Hellenistic values of knowledge, experience, and creativity, while the prophet Ahiah represents the Hebraic values of obedience and self-denial.

In both of these earlier novels, the Vridar character is the Hellenist. Rabi and Solomon are simply Vardis Fisher-type characters set imaginatively in different historical periods. The same is true of the main character of *The Island of the Innocent*: a wealthy Greek physician named Philemon. In most ways, Philemon epitomizes the Hellenistic worldview. He is well-educated, skeptical, intellectually curious, well-traveled, and a confirmed sensualist. However, when he is thrust into the middle of the pre-Maccabean conflict between the Hellenistic Jews and the *Hasidim*, or "pious Jews,"[17] Philemon chooses Hebraism—not out of any personal conviction or religious devotion, but out of love for a woman.

The first sentence of *The Island of the Innocent* introduces the reader to the obsessive love at the center of the novel: "He was Philemon, a Hellene, looking for a girl named Judith, a daughter of Israel, and he felt pretty absurd for having come down from Antioch because of an infatuation more than a year old."[18] Philemon had seen Judith only once, by chance in a crowd when she was twelve years old. As the novel begins, he is returning to Jerusalem to find her—and, in the process, to reunite with his Jewish friend Rueben, with whom he studied in Antioch. As soon as he arrives, however, Philemon is thrust into the conflict engulfing Jerusalem. Reuben is a leader of the Hellenistic Jews and is actively working with Antiochus IV and other forces within the Seleucid Empire to eliminate Jewish ritual and worship for good. Two of Judith's siblings—her brother Paul and her sister Angela—are among Reuben's most loyal followers, and her oldest brother, Hosah, is a leader of the pious Jews. Judith, who is only thirteen years old when the novel begins, is solidly within Hosah's sphere of influence.

While Philemon searches for Judith, he learns more about her strange and violent religion. Somewhat implausibly, Philemon has read many of the Jewish scriptures in the libraries at Antioch, but he has had little personal experience with the Jewish people. At the end of the first chapter, he watches helplessly as a Jewish crowd stones a man to death because he trespassed on ground considered sacred. He gets a close view of the "religious fanaticism in the seed of Abraham," and he is repulsed by it—as are many of the city's more secular Jews. Nevertheless, because of his love for Judith he tries to remain neutral in the internecine conflict developing around him. Finally, Judith's sister, Angela (the Greek name that she uses in place of her given name, Hepzibeth) tells Philemon that his studied neutrality cannot remain possible. "When the trouble comes," she warns, "when Jew kills Jew—when brother murders his brother, mother denies her daughter, and father slays his own son—when all that comes—and it's coming—whose side will you be on."[19]

This question initially perplexes Philemon, but, in the end, it is answered by default. When he rescues Judith from the High Priest Menelaus—a Hellenist favorite who intends to rape her—Philemon is imprisoned, renounced by his Hellenist friends, and embraced by the pious Jews, who soften to the idea of his marrying Judith, provided he undergo baptism and circumcision and become a Jew himself. By this time, Judith completely returns his affections. However, as Antiochus IV's persecutions become intolerable, and the Maccabean rebellion breaks out in the mountains, the happy (and the unhappy) festivities must be postponed. Through a combination of his passion for Judith and the whims of circumstance, Philemon finds himself a foot soldier in the revolutionary army of Judas the Maccabee. He has become a partisan in support of a religion that he does not accept. And he must fight to the death to support values and beliefs that he finds reprehensible.

Most of us, of course, will never be in a situation quite like this. If we take away the elements that make *The Island of the Innocent* a romantic adventure story, though, we are left with a dilemma that many people in religious organizations today will find eerily familiar. People today affiliate with religions for many reasons that do not include genuine conversion: family obligations, marital accommodation, social expectations, and so on. Much of the time this works out fine. And this can produce a profound cognitive dissonance among those who, for reasons that they do not entirely control, are part of a religious community whose core beliefs they reject or even find morally reprehensible. For the last third of the novel, Philemon struggles with precisely this kind of cognitive dissonance and must work to create a philosophy that reconciles his behavior with his beliefs.

To accomplish this reconciliation, Philemon reframes his affiliation with Judaism as an intellectual rather than a religious connection, and he invokes three arguments to justify his participation. First, in an internal monologue, he separates the practical good that Judaism does as a religious community from any evaluation of its truth claims. "There was treasure here," he told himself while observing a Sabbath meal. "Possibly mixed with it was much that was superstitious and evil; but there was good here and it was this good, this enrichment of hope, patience, and faith that Reuben and Angela would throw away, along with the tiresome nonsense in Leviticus."[20]

Second, in a conversation with the Hellenizers, Philemon argues that the unique doctrines of Judaism, while not true, at least provide a better moral framework than other doctrines:

> To believe in something higher and nobler than self . . . is to organize some kind of harmony—into an orderly and self-regulating power. It makes no difference at all, as I see it, whether there is a god—and of course there is not—as long as the idea of god serves the interests of harmony and design. All people but Jews have many gods; and they also have confusion, lack of symmetry and design and purpose, which is always found when there is no core, no center of control. Jews, with what seems to be superlative, even if unconscious, wisdom have refused to accept that disorder.[21]

When the Hellenizers call him out for promoting a religion that he knows to be false, Philemon makes his third major argument: that nothing is actually truer than anything else, so it doesn't really matter what one believes, as long as it works. "Who . . . can say what is false and what is not? Can any man?" he asks his companions before launching into a suspiciously modern defense of contingent truth:

> If we wait to be sure that a thing is right before casting our lives with it we'll never risk our lives for anything. Much of what Hosah believes is ridiculous to me but it serves him. Now he lies a beast in a cave, starving, but willing to die rather than renounce what is truth for him. And I find that good.
>
> Or I'd put it this way. . . . There's no God—we all agree on that; but in every man there is a god. If the man wants to think that his god is a being

or power somewhere out in space I can see no harm in it—or if he wants to think it is his own conscience or his own self-consciousness. As long as he has an idea that controls the caprices and tyrannies and impulses that would make him their slave.[22]

Philemon's moral reasoning here is hopelessly inappropriate for the time and the place of *The Island of the Innocent*. In the first place, the conflict between the Hellenists and the Hassidim is more political than religious. The pious Jews want to the right to impose a harsh theocracy on everybody in the community—and the right to stone infidels to death in the public square. The Hellenizers, on the other hand, want to make circumcision a capital offense and place a statue of Zeus in the temple. Philemon's bland moral relativism—what we might today call "Benign Whateverism"—has very little to offer to either side. Philemon has been thrust in the middle of an epic cultural clash that cannot be resolved simply by just letting everybody live by the truths that work for them. He and Judith do not live in the kind of society that could even understand the post-Enlightenment concept of religious pluralism.

But Vardis Fisher lived in a society that could understand it. The basic steps that he outlines through Philemon's intellectual journey—separating a religion's truth claims from its practical value, focusing on the positive social and familial aspects of a religious community, and rejecting the existence of any absolute truth upon which to ground religious belief—have made it possible for generations of nonbelievers to participate in religious communities whose doctrines they may reject and even find distasteful. They are, I would argue, some of the most important tools available for diaspora writers (Mormon or otherwise) who want to maintain connections to their religion and its culture—whether through personal participation in activities and rituals, through ties to loved ones and family members, or through public confession in the form of art or literature.

A Goat for Azazel: Religion as Research

The ninth novel of the *Testament of Man* begins in 64 CE, on the night of July 19—the night that Rome burned. On that fateful night, the novel's protagonist, a fourteen-year-old Roman boy named Damon, has been invited to attend a banquet given by Emperor Nero. As the banquet progresses, the guests begin to hear rumors of a great fire, and Damon rushes out to find his mother, who had converted to Christianity, the strange new religion said to be responsible for setting the fire in order to hasten the return of the Lord. Damon finds his mother dancing ecstatically with other Christians as Rome burns. She is so consumed by spiritual ecstasy that she does not recognize her only son. A few days later, however, his mother is among the Christians arrested for arson and sentenced to burn, and Damon tries, naïvely, to save her life. "What happened then," Fisher tells us, "he was to spend a lifetime trying to understand":

> She was enveloped in flames! An incredible thing then happened and Damon was to ask himself many times if he saw it clearly. Though the flames had risen to her breast she seemed not to be suffering at all. She was smiling at him. . . . His mother's whole face seemed to Damon to be radiant, to be suffused with a light not of this world. . . . She made no effort at all to free herself; she kept her gaze fixed on the heavens, looking for her Savior and Lord. This life did not matter, she said. My son be brave, she said to him. And there she died.[23]

Thus begins Damon's lifelong quest to understand the last moments of his mother's life. "What was it in this new faith that crowned a person with such nobility in her last moments of agony?" he asked.[24] This quest lasts from the first night of the great fire in the year 64 until his death almost fifty years later, when he is trampled to death by a mob while witnessing the death of another Christian martyr.[25] It takes him throughout the Roman world, to the pockets of Christians in Rome, Antioch, Corinth, Athens, and Alexandra. And it introduces him to many of the figures who shaped Christianity during its first and second generations, including two of the authors of the New Testament: the formidable pedagogue Luke, and the venerable apostle John. In each location, Damon encounters interlocutors who are able to discuss Christianity at great length and with perfect objectivity. From the literary perspective, this does not make for a great novel. *A Goat for Azazel* has less plot, and more philosophical discussion, than any other volume of *The Testament of Man*. What little story the novel has serves only as a scaffold for a 368-page history lecture—including more than 50 pages of notes at the end.

Read as a history lesson, however, *A Goat for Azazel* is not without interest. In his 50 years of traveling, Damon encounters two constant themes.

First, every group of Christians has its own doctrines and its own distinct understanding of Jesus Christ. Some believe Christ to have been a mortal who became a God and others saw him as a God who became a mortal. Some insisted that he was crucified by the Jews or the Romans just a few years into his ministry, while others believed that he died in bed after living a long life. There is, he discovers, no central authority, no consistent doctrine, no common vocabulary, and no consistent idea of what it means to be a Christian.

The second thing that Damon discovers is that practically nothing that any Christian sect believes is unique to Christianity. The idea of a Savior-God exists throughout the ancient world. Jesus is a reconfiguration of the Greek hero of Jason. The Virgin Mary is based on the Egyptian goddess Isis. The figure of Satan comes from the Zoroastrian counter-deity, Ahriman. Much of the proverbial wisdom that Matthew put into the mouth of Jesus comes from Buddha, Lao Tzu, and the other great sages of the ancient Far East. And the most distinctive Christian doctrine of all—the belief that Christ died to atone for the sins of those who accept him—comes straight from the Hebrew ritual of the scapegoat. In this ritual, which gives the novel its title, the priest designates one goat for the Lord and one for the demon Azazel. The Lord's goat is sacrificed, while the goat for Azazel is loaded with the sins of the people and sent into the wilderness.[26] As Damon interviews Christian after Christian, he discovers that the only doctrine that unifies them is that Jesus Christ somehow became the human equivalent of Azazel's goat.

At the end of the book, Damon settles down to raise a family and write a book about Christianity. Years pass before he hears that Ignatius, the Bishop of Antioch whom he had met years earlier, has been arrested and taken to Rome to be tried and (most likely) executed. He decides to follow the soon-to-be martyr to "see if his faith sustains him the way it sustained my mother."[27] Damon becomes part of the crowd that watches Ignatius travel from Antioch to Rome in the custody of Roman soldiers, addressing Christians at every stop. He watches as a patient Roman captain tells him that he can go free if only he will swear loyalty to Caesar; when he refuses, he is condemned to die by fire. As Damon watches him burn to death, while frenzied spectators cheer, he experiences a sympathetic conversion to Christianity:

Damon could look for only a moment at the horrible sight. The flames had completely enveloped him, there was fire in his hair and beard. He was there, he was not bound and he had not moved. Damon then forced himself to look once again at the faces that were not human and he hated them and he recognized in this moment that he was a Christian, as he would have been a Jew if he had been present when the holy city was sacked; as he would be in any situation of torture what was dearest on earth to the one tortured. Was that not what it all meant?[28]

Moments later, the crowd tramples Damon to death while he is pondering his connection to the dying Bishop of Antioch.

The final chapter of *A Goat for Azazel* consists almost entirely of passages from Damon's book about Christianity read by his son. In it, he shares the fruits of a lifetime of research on his mother's faith. The book documents the rise of Christianity from a "mystery cult, offering salvation by supernatural means" to a "sacramental cult, which then took Greek ideas into its doctrines." It explains how the Christian cult almost immediately fragmented into mutually exclusive regional cults. And it painstakingly traces the pagan myths that became part of the Jesus story: "they have their Lord resurrected from a rock tomb, like Mithra; turn water into wine, like Dionysus; walk on the waves, like Poseidon; lie in a manger, like Ion; come to birth in a stable, like Horus; and from a virgin mother, as with all the gods."[29]

We find nothing in Damon's book that confirms his end-of-life affirmation of Christianity—except for the fact that he wrote it and that he spent most of his life trying to understand how Christianity gave his mother the strength to embrace her martyrdom. And he never comes to a satisfactory answer. His book explains the history of Christianity and the development of its doctrine, but it captures nothing about the extraordinary faith of the Christian martyrs. And his final conversion comes as the result of human sympathy rather than faith or understanding. But it is not his faith or understanding that defines Damon as part of an intellectual diaspora: it is the fact that he continues to search—that he feels an irresistible pull to understand his mother's religion—in which he has seen something remarkable that he cannot explain away.

And so it has always been with the writers of the Mormon diaspora—those and the dozens of other writers and scholars who rejected much of Mormon doctrine, practice, or culture but were driven to study it and write about it for much of their lives. This would include such figures as Virginia Sorensen, who gave up Mormonism and became an Anglican but wrote a half a dozen novels about both historical and contemporary Mormonism.[30] It includes Juanita Brooks and Maurine Whipple, who suffered the ostracism of their fellow Saints for their historical and fictional writings about controversial elements of Mormon history,[31] and Samuel Taylor, who wrote such classics as *Nightfall at Nauvoo*, *Family Kingdom*, and *The Kingdom or Nothing* largely to understand the Church that excommunicated his father.[32] And it applies to Vardis Fisher, who wrote the world's first serious treatment of the Mormon story in fiction. Like so many of his literary creations, Fisher struggled to understand the religion and culture that produced him and sustained his loved ones.

As much as Fisher rejected religion's norms and historical truth claims, he never found a nonreligious vocabulary capable of describing himself to himself or of communicating his thoughts to the rest of the world. For nearly all of his life, Vardis Fisher occupied the position that he attributed to Vridar Hunter in *We Are Betrayed*, the third book of the tetralogy: "He felt desolate and empty because he had lost something; he was adrift from his people and his Church and he had found nothing to take their place."[33] This perspective of someone who simultaneously needs and rejects religious faith soon became the lens through which Fisher analyzed religion, philosophy, and the human condition. Like Vridar, he "pondered the matter and searched books, [and] saw the birth and growth of a strange, yet very anxious, phenomenon."[34]

Fisher eventually settled on the name *orphan* to describe this phenomenon and incorporated this term into his *Orphans in Gethsemane*, a revision of the tetralogy that also became the final volume of the *Testament of Man*. An orphan, of course, is a person defined primarily by an absence. Literally, an orphan is somebody who lacks parents. When used as a religious or philosophical term, it suggests somebody who is defined primarily by the absence of belief or metaphysical certainty. Fisher's most ambitious project—the twelve-volume *Testament of Man* series—attempts to explain the religious and philosophical systems that shaped orphans like himself through the cultures they created.

Each of the texts discussed at length in this book—the Antelope novels, *Children of God*, and the *Testament of Man* series—forms part of the much larger project of Fisher's life work of explaining himself by tracing the history of the ideas that shaped his intellect and defined his world-view, even as he actively rejected them. The project began with a series of novels based on his own life and continued with an epic novel about the religious tradition that shaped him the most. With *Children of God*, Fisher began something like the kind of genealogy work that Mormons have long practiced in conjunction with the vicarious ordinances in their temples. But instead of tracing his physical ancestors, he traced the ancestors of his ideas back to the world of his grandfather and great-grandfather, who crossed the plains with Brigham Young. In the *Testament of Man* series, Fisher completed the intellectual genealogy that he began with *Children of God*. In the process, he demonstrated that religion can define a work by its absence just as it can by its presence.

And this is the final reason that Fisher's status as a Mormon writer—and, indeed as the first important Mormon writer and the logical start-ing point for a canon of Mormon literature—does not require us to posit that he believed in or practiced a Mormon faith. Yes, Fisher wrote about Mormonism by name in about a third of his novels, culminating in his epic treatment of the migration from Nauvoo to the Great Basin. And he also deployed identifiably Mormon rhetorical strategies—such as creating "another testament" of the Bible or writing a genealogy of his ideas—as organizing principles for his major works. But both of these elements of his writing are peripheral, and Fisher was Mormon to his core—by his own standard of evaluating his core—because it was part of the cultural and intellectual heritage in which he lived and worked. For nearly all of his adult life, Vardis Fisher was a religious unbeliever; of this there can be little doubt. But Mormonism was the religion that he didn't believe in—and this fact had profound implications for his work as a writer.

A Bibliographic Essay

Primary Works

Vardis Fisher wrote 26 novels, of which 25 fit more or less easily into one of three categories: 1) seven Antelope Novels (including the tetralogy); 2) six Western historical novels; and 3) the twelve-volume *Testament of Man* series. He also wrote several works of nonfiction and published volumes of short stories, poems, and occasional pieces, for a total of 37 published books.

Antelope Novels

Toilers of the Hills (Houghton Mifflin, 1928)
Dark Bridwell (Houghton Mifflin, 1931)
In Tragic Life (Caxton/Doubleday, Doran, 1932)
Passions Spin the Plot (Caxton/Doubleday, Doran, 1934)
We Are Betrayed (Caxton/Doubleday, Doran, 1935)
No Villain Need Be (Caxton/Doubleday, Doran, 1936)
April: A Fable of Love (Caxton/Doubleday, Doran, 1937)

Novels of the Vridar Hunter Tetralogy

Fisher's first seven novels are all set in the same fictional world called Antelope—the actual name of the region in Idaho where Fisher grew up. Fisher's Antelope functions as a coherent storyworld like William Faulkner's Yoknapatawpha (which Faulkner began creating the year after *Toilers of the Hills* was published) or Thomas Hardy's Wessex (to which Fisher's early novels were routinely compared). Four of the Antelope novels—*In Tragic Life, Passions Spin the Plot, We Are Betrayed*, and *No Villain Need Be*—constitute an autobiographical tetralogy, whose main character, Vridar Hunter, functions as a fictionalized version of Fisher himself. Vridar also occurs as a minor character in *Dark Bridwell*, and his uncle and aunt—Dock and Opal Hunter—are the heroes of *Toilers of the Hills*. *Dark Bridwell* was issued by Pyramid Books in a paperback volume under the title *The Wild Ones* in 1952.

In addition to these novels, seven of the previously published stories collected in *Love and Death* are set in the Antelope storyworld: "The Mother" (1933), "The Scarecrow" (1934), "Joe Burt's Wife" (1934), "The Legend of Red Hair" (1935), "Laughter" (1936), "Charivari" (1939), and "The Storm" (1947). Between 1928 to 1931, Fisher also published several collections of Antelope character sketches in sonnet form, inspired by Edgar Lee Masters's *Spoon River Anthology*. A total of ten poems appeared, some more than once, in contemporary poetry magazines and anthologies—usually under the collective title "Antelope People."[1] These poems created brief snapshots of characters that would later appear—usually in minor roles—in the Antelope stories and novels.

The novels, stories, and poems set in Antelope never found a larger readership, but they did attract significant critical attention, largely because they paired well with the work of Southern writers such as Faulkner, Thomas Wolfe, and Erskine Caldwell and allowed critics to analyze a broader regional movement reminiscent of Hardy's work at the end of the prior century. Fisher, though, steadfastly resisted attempts to put his work in a critical box. "I published a novel laid in that hill country, a second, a third, never dreaming that certain reviewers would be filing me away under "Hardy" or "Wessex," he wrote after abandoning the Antelope setting. "The reviewers never understood that I detested Antelope country and was trying to come to some kind of terms with it, so that I could proceed to a more sunlit area."[2]

Western Historical Novels

Children of God: An American Epic (Harper, 1939)
City of Illusion (Harper, 1941)
The Mothers: An American Saga of Courage (Vanguard, 1943)
Pemmican: A Novel of the Hudson's Bay Company (Doubleday, 1956)
Tale of Valor: A Novel of the Lewis and Clark Expedition (Doubleday, 1958)
Mountain Man: A Novel of Male and Female in the Early American West (Morrow, 1965)

Though Fisher himself took these Western-themed novels less seriously than his other fiction, they provided much of his income as a writer and are responsible for most of his continuing reputation fifty years after his death. And the most influential of all are the first and the last. *Children of God*, a three-generation epic story of the Mormon pioneers, won the Harper Prize in 1939 and allowed Fisher to purchase the property in Hangerman, Idaho, where he lived for the rest of his life. *Mountain Man*, a novel based on the exploits of Jeremiah "Liver Eating" Johnson, had only modest sales when it was published in 1965. However, after Fisher died, it became a best seller when it was used as the basis for the Robert Redford movie *Jeremiah Johnson* in 1972.

Fisher's five other historical novels each dealt with specific events in Western American or Canadian history. *City of Illusion* chronicles the discovery of the Comstock Lode—a large deposit of silver near Virginia City, Nevada, in 1859. *The Mothers* tells the tale of the Donner Party's ill-fated journey through the Sierra Nevada Mountains in 1846. *Pemmican* explores the war between trading companies in Canada's Hudson Bay Colony between 1815 and 1821. *Tale of Valor* narrates the famous Lewis and Clark expedition to the Pacific coast that began in 1804. Fisher conducted extensive research for each of these novels and received strong praise from critics for their historical accuracy.

The Testament of Man

1. *Darkness and the Deep* (Vanguard, 1943)
2. *The Golden Rooms* (Vanguard, 1944)
3. *Intimations of Eve* (Vanguard, 1946)
4. *Adam and the Serpent* (Vanguard, 1947)
5. *The Divine Passion* (Vanguard, 1948)
6. *The Valley of Vision* (Abelard, 1951)
7. *The Island of the Innocent* (Abelard, 1952)
8. *Jesus Came Again: A Parable* (Swallow, 1956)
9. *A Goat for Azazel* (Swallow, 1956)
10. *Peace Like a River* (Swallow, 1957)
11. *My Holy Satan* (Swallow, 1958)
12. *Orphans in Gethsemane* (Swallow, 1960)

Fisher worked on the *Testament of Man* series for nearly 20 years, through poor sales and disputes with publishers, because he saw it as his most significant body of work. He also saw the *Testament* as a logical extension of his own autobiographical tetralogy. In the tetralogy, Fisher tried to understand himself by examining his childhood. In the *Testament of Man*, he tried to understand himself by exploring the origins of the ideas that shaped him and his society.

The history of *Testament of Man* divides into four uneven groups, each narrowing the portion of humanity's ancestry that it describes. The first four novels can all be characterized as prehistorical. *Darkness of the Deep* takes place millions of years ago in the human evolutionary past, while *The Golden Rooms* imagines the conflict between our Cro-Magnon forebears and their and Neanderthal rivals around 40,000 years ago. The next two novels—*Intimations of Eve* and *Adam and the Serpent*—take place right before the dawn of recorded history and chronicle human society's transformation from a matriarchal to a patriarchal order through the intervention of a primitive form of the Hebrew religion.

The next three novels treat the development of Judaism during roughly the same period covered by the Old Testament. *The Divine Passion* contains a heavily demythologized version of Genesis and Exodus among a small, patriarchal tribe in the Levant. After publishing this book, Fisher's publisher, Vanguard, dropped the series due to both disappointing sales and discomfort about the possibility of religious objections to the coming books. Abelard Press picked up the series for *The Valley of Vision*, a fictional biography of Solomon and the conflict between kings and prophets in early Hebrew society. Abelard also published *The Island of the Innocent*, a love story between a Greek man and a Jewish woman during the time of the Maccabean revolt.

The next four novels treated the origin and development of Christianity. *Jesus Came Again*, the eighth novel in the series, portrayed Jesus as a non-divine, well-intentioned traveling philosopher who originally rejects the role of Messiah but comes to accept it because he realizes that his disciples need to believe in him. The follow-up, *A Goat for Azazel*, explores the different forms of Jesus-worship in the first generation after Christ's death. *Peace like a River* (published in paperback under the title *The Passion Within*) takes place a few hundred years later among the desert-dwelling Christian ascetics. The final Christian novel, *My Holy Satan* is set in Medieval Europe at the time of the Inquisition.

The fourth category in the *Testament of Man* is the single book, *Orphans in Gethsemane*, which rewrites and extends the four novels of the tetralogy. By placing Vridar Hunter's story at the end of the series, Fisher highlights the way that the ideas about sexuality, religion, and creativity that he explored in the series impacted his own development as a human being and a writer. *Orphans* is several times longer than any of the other books in the series—so long that it had to be published as two paperback novels: *For Passion, For Heaven* and *The Great Confession*.

Other Books

Sonnets to an Imaginary Madonna (Harold Vinal, 1927)
The Neurotic Nightingale (Casanova Press, 1935)
*Idaho: A Guide in Word and Picture (Caxton Printers, 1937)
*The Idaho Encyclopedia (Caxton Printers, 1938)
Forgive Us Our Virtues (Caxton Printers, 1938)
*Idaho Lore (Caxton Printers, 1939)
The Caxton Printers of Idaho (Society of Bibliosophers, 1944)
God or Caesar: The Writing of Fiction for Beginners (Caxton Printers, 1953)
Love and Death (Doubleday, 1959)
Suicide or Murder: The Strange Death of Governor Meriwether Lewis (Swallow, 1962)
Thomas Wolfe as I Knew Him (Swallow, 1963)
‡*Gold Rushes and Mining Camps of the Early American West* (Caxton Printers, 1968)
   *Published by the Federal Writers' Project with Fisher as primary author
   ‡Coauthored with Opal Laurel Holmes

Like most writers of stature, Fisher published a number of collections, work-for-hire, and idiosyncratic personal projects over his long career. This miscellaneous category includes *Forgive Us Our Virtues*, a psychological satire novel that does not fit into one of the categories so far. It also includes a beginner's guide to writing novels (*God or Caesar*), a tribute to the Caxton Printers, and his poetry book *Sonnets to an Imaginary Madonna*—a vanity project for which he paid $400. This category also includes the three volumes that he produced as the director of the Federal Writers' Project in Idaho.

Three of Fisher's books are collections of previously published work: *The Neurotic Nightingale* and *Thomas Wolfe as I Knew Him* collect nonfiction essays from magazines and journals, and *Love and Death* collected all of his published short fiction, including "The Odyssey of a Hero," which was originally published in a separate volume with limited distribution by Ritten House Press in 1937.

Toward the end of his life, Fisher published two nonfiction works that grew out of his extensive research into the history of the American West.

Suicide or Murder examined the death of Meriwether Lewis, one of the heroes of *Tale of Valor*. *Gold Rushes and Mining Camps of the Early American West* was a guidebook, lavishly illustrated with photographs, which he wrote with his third wife Opal Laurel Holmes and published just months before his death.

Opal Laurel Holmes Imprint

After Fisher died, his widow, Opal Laurel Holmes, created an imprint—Opal Laurel Holmes, Publisher—to reissue the books of Fisher's for which she held the copyright. Between 1970 and 1981, she republished five books under this imprint: *The Mothers* (1970), *Children of God* (1975), *Pemmican* (1976), *Dark Bridwell* (1979), and *Sonnets to an Imaginary Madonna* (1981). After her dispute with Leonard Arrington and the Church of Jesus Christ of Latter-day Saints over Fisher's connection to Mormonism, she appended the press release "Vardis Fisher Was Not a Mormon" and her open letter to Spencer W. Kimball to the end of every book she printed.

Newspaper and Magazine Articles

In addition to his fiction and nonfiction writing, Fisher published hundreds of editorial columns in Idaho newspapers. Between 1941 and 1946, he wrote a weekly column for the *Idaho Statesman* which, in 1945, appeared under the title "Objection Overruled." In July of 1946, he resigned from the *Statesman* after an editorial dispute and began writing a column titled "Vardis Fisher Says" for the *Idaho Pioneer Statewide*. This column was soon syndicated throughout the state, and he continued to write it for the rest of his life.

Most of Fisher's significant magazine and journal articles are collected in *Thomas Wolfe as I Knew Him and Other Essays*. One of the most significant essays not in the volume—at least for scholars of Fisher and Mormons—is his essay "The Mormons," published in the British magazine *Transatlantic* (May 1944, 37–41). In this essay, Fisher gives a brief overview of Mormon history and depicts Salt Lake City as a thoroughly modern urban space. Echoing his views in the final section of *Children of God*, he concludes that Mormonism, once interesting and transgressive, had settled in to become "merely another . . . of the Protestant sects" (41).

Fisher also published three significant journal articles after *Thomas Wolfe as I Knew Him*. The first of these, "Vardis Fisher Comments on His 'Testament of Man' Series," appeared in a special issue of *American Book*

Collector dedicated to his work (*American Book Collector* XIV [September 1963], 31–36. And he contributed two articles consisting of his observations about the state of Western American literature. The first of these was part of a symposium hosted by the *South Dakota Review* (Issue II, Autumn 1964, 19–23), which consisted of his printed response to a series of questions sent to him by the editors. The second, "The Western Writer and the Eastern Establishment" appeared in *Western American Literature* I (Winter 1967): 244–59.

Papers and Unpublished Manuscripts

The bulk of Vardis Fisher's papers are located in two university special collections. The larger of these, the Vardis Fisher Papers at Yale University (YCAL MSS 555) contain his correspondence with agents and publishers, personal correspondence, miscellaneous writings, photographs, audiocassettes, and miscellaneous material.

The Boise State University Library houses seven distinct collections relevant to Fisher and his work: the Fisher Family Papers (MSS 160), the Vardis and Opal Fisher Papers (MSS 159), the Joseph M. Flora Papers (MSS 285), the Mabel Clore Collection on Vardis Fisher (MSS 002), the George E. Brown Jr. Correspondence with Vardis Fisher (MSS 169), the Lloyd Jensen Collection on Vardis Fisher (MSS 269), and the Dorys Crow Grover Papers and Collections on Vardis Fisher and Ernest Hemingway (MSS 120).

A small but significant collection of early Fisher family letters is housed at Brigham Young University-Idaho (MSSI 5), and smaller collections of material relevant to Fisher's work can be found at the University of Utah (MS0401), Weber State University (MS 134), the University of Idaho (Manuscript Group 2180), Utah State University (USU_MSS 350) and Washington State University (Cage 229). A collection of letters between Fisher and his agent Elizabeth Nowell is contained in the Thomas Wolfe collection at the University of North Carolina, Chapel Hill (CW2.1). The L. Tom Perry Special Collections Room at Brigham Young University-Provo holds a single bound volume containing five one-act plays that Fisher wrote as an undergraduate but never published and cannot be found elsewhere (MS 1436).

A final primary source for studying Vardis Fisher is an interview that literary editor John R. Milton conducted with Fisher in April of 1967. The interview discusses Fisher's history, his Mormon heritage, his *Testament of Man* series, and his general thoughts on literature and society. A video of the interview can be accessed on the Internet at https://www.youtube.com/watch?v=UTYnd2f5wYc, and it was published in 1972 as *Three West: Conversations with Vardis Fisher, Max Evans, Michael Straight*, ed., John R. Milton (Vermillion: Dakota Press, University of South Dakota, 1972, 1–45).

Secondary Works
Bibliographies

George Kellog's "Vardis Fisher: A Bibliography" (Western American Literature 5, no. 1 [Spring 1970]: 45–64) provides an exhaustive catalog of published work by and about Vardis Fisher, including foreign and paperback editions of his books, book chapters and magazine articles by Fisher, and reviews of his books in the national and international press. Completed two years after Fisher's death, Kellog's bibliography remains a useful guide to Fisher's primary work, exempting only his newspaper columns. It is also a reasonably complete guide to scholarship and criticism about Fisher through 1970.

A more recent, and equally exhaustive, bibliography appears in Martin Kirch's *Western American Novelists, Volume 1: Walter van Tilburg Clark, Dan Cushman, H. L. Davis, Vardis Fisher, A. B. Guthrie Jr., William Humphrey, and Dorothy M. Johnson* (New York: Garland Pub, 1995, 292–519). Kirch's bibliography includes nearly everything that is in Kellog's earlier work, with an additional 25 years of secondary material. Kirch also annotates nearly all of the secondary sources about Fisher, some of them quite extensively. Kirch's coverage of Mormon regionalism in which Fisher plays a major part is uneven. He includes, for example, Edward Geary's essay "Women Regionalists of Mormon Country," which mentions Fisher only once and in passing, but he misses the same author's "The Poetics of Provincialism: Mormon Regional Fiction" and "Mormondom's Lost Generation: The Novelists of the 1940s," both of which treat Fisher extensively.[3]

A third bibliography of Fisher's work, Mark Canada's "Vardis Fisher: An Essay in Bibliography," appears as the final chapter of *Rediscovering Vardis Fisher: Centennial Essays* (Caldwell: University of Idaho Press, 2000, 209–34). Canada's essay lacks the exhaustive detail of earlier bibliographies but includes much more context and evaluation of the sources.

Books

In eighty years, only a handful of books have been published about Vardis Fisher, and only a few of those are useful for scholars. Three of them could reasonably be called indispensable for those who want an understanding of Fisher's life, career, and reputation. The most useful monograph is Joseph M. Flora's *Vardis Fisher* (New York: Twayne, 1965), published as part of Twayne's United States Authors Series. This book, based partly on Flora's dissertation at the University of Michigan, focuses heavily on the tetralogy and its recreation in *Orphans in Gethsemane*. It also includes chapters on his Antelope novels and his Western Americana. The book established Flora as the 20th century's pre-eminent Fisher scholar, and it remains the best starting place for those interested in an academic study of his work.

Thirty-five years later, Flora assembled a collection of essays reevaluating Fisher's work for the edited volume *Rediscovering Vardis Fisher*. Though now twenty years old, this collection is the last attempt by scholars to grapple with Fisher's legacy in a systematic way. It offers twelve essays primarily by scholars of Western literature, including a feminist analysis of *The Mothers*, an evaluation of Fisher's characterizations of Native Americans, an analysis of the controversy about his Mormon roots, and an anthropological evaluation of *The Testament of Man*.

The third essential book—the only full-length biography of Fisher ever written—is Tim Woodward's *Tiger on the Road* (Caldwell, ID: Caxton Printers, 1989) by Idaho journalist Tim Woodward. Woodward interviewed many of Fisher's living friends and family members to put together the broad outline of his life and major work. Woodward's biography leaves much to be wished for. It is very lightly sourced and does not have an index, and it frequently gets details wrong by over-relying on Fisher's confessional novels for biographical details. But it is the only book-length biography of Fisher available, and it contains information from the author's personal correspondence that can be found nowhere else.

The second tier of books on Fisher are all either article-length publications that have been bound as books or unrevised dissertations with extremely limited distribution. The first group includes *Vardis Fisher: A Critical Summary with Notes on His Life and Personality* (Caldwell, ID: Caxton Printers, 1939), a twenty-page advertising booklet created by Caxton Printers as a promotional mailer in 1939 and reprinted in 1981 by an

Oregon firm called Authors of the West. It also includes Allan Crandall's self-published *Fisher of the Antelope Hills* (Manhattan, KS: Crandall Press, 1949), Wayne Chatterton's *Vardis Fisher: Frontier and Regional Works* (Boise State College Western Writers Series #1, 1972), and the very strange, vaguely Marxist book *Vardis Fisher: Challenge to Evasion* by David Rein (Chicago: Normandie Press, 1938), for which Fisher himself wrote the foreword.

Fisher's work, and especially the *Testament of Man*, became a modestly popular subject for PhD dissertations in English in the 1960s and 1970s. In 1972, the Revisionist Press of New York began soliciting dissertations on Fisher, which they published without revision or even new typesetting—simply by photocopying the original dissertations and binding them in a red cover. Four dissertations were published in this way: Dorys C. Grover's *Vardis Fisher: The Novelist as Poet* (1973); Alfred K. Thomas's *The Epic of Evolution, Its Etiology and Art: A Study of Vardis Fisher's Testament of Man* (1973); George F. Day's *The Uses of History in the Novels of Vardis Fisher* (1976); and Lester Strong's *The Past in the Present: Two Essays on History and Myth in Vardis Fisher's Testament of Man*. A fifth book, *A Solitary Voice: Vardis Fisher: A Collection of Essays*, also by Dorys C. Grover, was published in 1973.

In addition to these books, two special issues of periodicals function as edited volumes, or collections of essays dedicated entirely to Vardis Fisher. The first of these is a special Vardis Fisher issue of *The American Book Collector* (XIV, no. 1 [September] 1963), which includes critical essays, career retrospectives, a piece by Fisher called "The Novelist and His Characters," and the essay "Once in a Wifetime" by Fisher's wife Opal Laurel Holmes.

The second is the first and only issue of the *Vardis Fisher Newsletter*, edited by Mick McCallister and published by Dancing Badger Press in 1990. This issue features two articles by McCallister, a review of Woodward's *Tiger on the Road*, and several reassessments of Fisher's novels—including an evaluation of *Jesus Came Again* by the noted Mormon theologian and philosophy professor Sterling M. McMurrin.

Articles and Book Chapters

Around two hundred articles and book chapters about Vardis Fisher were published between 1930 and 1995 and catalogued in the Kirch bibliography. The subjects of these articles vary widely, but two important themes recur throughout them: 1) critical examinations of Fisher's role in creating a genuine regional literature in the American West; and 2) articles by Latter-day Saint scholars and students of Mormonism interested in situating Fisher within Mormonism and Mormon literature. The bulk of the essays in the first group were published in the 1930s and 1940s, when regional scholars in the West were trying to construct a canon of texts that could be considered Western literature. Most of the essays in the second group come from the 1960s and 1970s, when Mormon scholars were trying to do much the same thing.

The Western regional scholarship includes the work of some of the 20th century's most important literary critics, such as John Peale Bishop's "The Strange Case of Vardis Fisher" (*Southern Review* III [Autumn 1937]: 348–59) and Carl Van Doren's *The American Novel* (Macmillan, 1940, 363–64). It also includes George D. Snell's *Shapers of American Fiction, 1798–1947* (Dutton, 1947, 263–88), which pairs Fisher and Erskine Caldwell as exemplars of, respectively, Southern and Western naturalism. And it includes Ray B. West's *Writing in the Rocky Mountains* (University of Nebraska Press, 1947), which discusses Fisher in three of its four chapters. The final chapter of West's book, "Mormon Material in Serious Fiction" (404–13), examines Fisher in the context of Mormon literature, bridging the important gap between Western regional and Mormon fiction.

The fact that Fisher was raised in the Mormon Church and wrote one of the most popular novels ever written about Mormonism made it inevitable that he would attract the attention of Mormon scholars when they began to study Mormon Literature. This work began in 1942, soon after prominent Utah historian Dale Morgan published two articles about contemporary novels that featured Fisher's work: "Mormon Storytellers" (*Rocky Mountain Review* 7 [Fall 1942]: 1, 3–7); and "Fisher and Snell. Mormon Story Tellers" (*Rocky Mountain Reader*, ed. Ray B. West Jr. [New York: Dutton, 1946, 404–13]). West saw Fisher as a crucial figure in creating the market for Mormon stories in the broader American public sphere. Another Mormon historian, David Brion Davis, published a paper in 1953 that catalogued historical inaccuracies in *Children of God* ("Children of God: An Historian's Evaluation," *Western Humanities Review* VIII [Winter 1953]: 49–56).

More than twenty years after Morgan first broached the topic, Joseph Flora contributed the article "Vardis Fisher and the Mormons" to one of the early issues *Dialogue: A Journal of Mormon Thought* (4 no.3 [Autumn 1969]: 48–55). Flora reworked this essay to create the introduction to Opal Laurel

Holmes' reissue of *Children of God* in 1975. One year earlier, two Latter-day Saint English professors had included the first chapter of *Children of God* in *A Believing People* (Provo, UT: Brigham Young University Press, 1974), the first-ever anthology of Mormon Literature, which was used to teach the subject at BYU.

In 1976, a group of Latter-day Saint scholars created the Association for Mormon Letters, which aimed to promote scholarly discussion of important literature by and about Mormons. In the first meeting of the group, Ed Geary, professor of English at Brigham Young University, gave the paper "The Poetics of Provincialism: Mormon Regional Fiction," which identified Fisher—along with George Dixon Snell, Maurine Whipple, and Virginia Sorensen—as part of a cohort of mid-century Mormon writers who pioneered regional literature with a distinctively Mormon flavor. The paper was published in the proceedings of the conference in *Dialogue: A Journal of Mormon Thought* 11, no. 2 (Summer 1978): 15–25. Geary published another paper in 1978, which coined the term "Lost Generation" in reference to these and other mid-century regional writers ("Mormondom's Lost Generation: The Novelists of the 1940s," *BYU Studies Quarterly* 18, no. 1 [1978]: 89–98).

The most well-known and controversial of the Mormon Literature articles of the 1970s was the "The Mormon Heritage of Vardis Fisher," by Leonard Arrington and John Haupt (*BYU Studies* 18, no. 1 [1977]: 27–47), which argued that Fisher never abandoned the LDS Church and remained fundamentally Mormon for his entire life. This essay drew the wrath of Fisher's widow, Opal Laurel Holmes, who issued the press release "Vardis Fisher Was Not a Mormon" and published it in each of the five Fisher books that she released under her own imprint.

Mick McCallister, a Fisher scholar who corresponded frequently with Holmes, delivered a scholarly rebuttal to Arrington and Haupt at the 1983 meeting of the Association for Mormon Letters. The paper, "Vardis Fisher's Mormon Heritage Re-Examined: A Critical Response," is available on McCallister's website, Wanderer's Well, at http://www.dancingbadger.com/vfmormonf.htm (November 2001).

By the mid-1980s, the initial burst of energy that accompanied the birth of the academic study of Mormon Literature had died down, and, with it, the critical discussion of Vardis Fisher—though the term "Lost Generation" to describe Fisher and other mid-century Mormon writers continued to play an important role as the third of four periods described in Eugene

England's influential taxonomy of Mormon Literature (see "Mormon Literature Progress and Prospects" in *Mormon Americana: A Guide to Sources and Collections in the United States* (*BYU Studies*, 1995: 455–505). Stephen L. Tanner's "Vardis Fisher and the Mormons" in *Rediscovering Vardis Fisher* (2000), 97–113, refers to nearly all of these previous articles and tries to situate them in a view that Fisher was culturally, but not religiously, Mormon.

Very little has been published about Fisher's literary work since the 2000 retrospective. But, as Fisher's life intersected with the lives of many people who became notable, he remains relevant to historians and biographers as a supporting character. For example, a chapter on Fisher's work with the Federal Writers' Project in Idaho appears in David Taylor's book *Soul of a People: the WPA Writers' Project Uncovers Depression America* (Hoboken, NJ: John Wiley & Sons, 2009, 97–109). Another chapter on Fisher, titled simply "Vardis," appears in W. Dale Nelson's biography of Alan Swallow: *Alan Swallow: Quality Publishing in the West* (Syracuse, NY: Syracuse University Press, 2010, 123–30). Steven Dillon discusses Fisher's use of the matriarchy myth in *Wolf-women and Phantom Ladies: Female Desire in 1940s US Culture* (Albany, NY: SUNY Press, 2016, 99–103). Fisher also makes minor appearances in recent books about Meriwether Lewis, Robert Redford, and Idaho culture.[4]

Writing about Fisher's Mormon background appeared only sporadically in the first two decades of the 21st century and includes brief analyses of *Children of God* in Dan Moos's *Outside America* (Lebanon, NH: UPNE, 2005, 137–40) and Terryl Givens's *People of Paradox* (New York: Oxford University Press, 2007, 287–88). It also includes my own essay, "Vardis Fisher's Mormon Scars: Mapping the Diaspora in *Testament of Man*" (*Dialogue: A Journal of Mormon Thought* 47, no. 3 [Fall 2014]: 1–22)—which forms the basis of Chapter 4 of the present work. Yet, as Mormon Studies comes into its own as an academic discipline, Fisher will likely be seen as an increasingly important historical figure and as one of the main points of contact between Mormonism and American culture during the middle years of the 20th century.

Notes

Chapter One. "Vardis Fisher Was Not a Mormon"

1. Leonard J. Arrington and John Haupt. "The Mormon Heritage of Vardis Fisher," *BYU Studies* 18, no. 1 (1977): 28. Three years later, Arrington and Davis Bitton, made a much weaker version of this claim in *The Mormon Experience* (New York: Knopf, 1979), arguing only that Fisher's Mormon upbringing had "a powerful influence" on both *Children of God*, Fisher's epic novel of the Mormon migration, and on much of his other fiction as well (330).

2. Vardis Fisher to Gilbert Rabin (promotion director at Abelard Press), June 12, 1951. Vardis Fisher Papers. Yale Collection of American Literature, Beinecke Rare Book and Manuscript Library, MSS 555, Box 24.

3. Vardis Fisher to Elizabeth Nowell, June 5, 1939. Vardis Fisher Papers. Yale Collection of American Literature, Beinecke Rare Book and Manuscript Library. MSS 555, Box 25. Underlining in original.

4. In his autobiographical novel, *In Tragic Life*, Fisher's fictional alter ego, Vridar Hunter, actually received a mission call to Spain, and he agonizes for days about whether or not to accept it. Fisher portrays Vridar's rejection of the mission call as a final rejection of the Church. I have not found evidence that Fisher himself received such a call, but the details of Vridar's life during this period do correspond to Fisher's own life in most regards. *In Tragic Life*, Caldwell, ID: Caxton Printers, 1932, 444–64.

5. For an account of James Strang's Beaver Island Kingdom, see Vickie Cleverley Speek's *God Has Made Us a Kingdom: James Strang and the Midwest Mormons* (Salt Lake City, UT: Signature Books, 2006) and Roger van Noord's *King of Beaver Island: The Life and Assassination of James Jesse Strang* (Urbana: University of Illinois Press, 1988).

6. John R. Milton, Vardis Fisher, Max Evans, and Michael W. Straight. *Three*

West: Conversations with Vardis Fisher, Max Evans, Michael Straight. Vermillion: Dakota Press, University of South Dakota, 1972, 3.

7. Vardis Fisher. "Hometown Revisited," in *Thomas Wolfe as I Knew Him and Other Essays*. Denver, CO: Alan Swallow, 1963, 119.

8. Ibid.

9. Interview with Irene Fisher Mead, January 1984, qtd. in Tim Woodward, *Tiger on the Road*. Caldwell, ID: Caxton Printers, 1989, 12.

10. Fisher, "My Biblical Heritage," in *Thomas Wolfe*, 161.

11. Arrington and Haupt, "Mormon Heritage," 31.

12. Woodward, *Tiger*, 44.

13. Fisher, *In Tragic Life*, 460–64. This book, and the three other autobiographical novels that followed it were reworked to form *Orphans in Gethsemane* (Denver, CO: Swallow, 1960), where the scene cited occurs on p. 222.

14. Arrington and Haupt, "Mormon Heritage," 32.

15. On October 1, 1915, Fisher wrote to his parents that: ""I have done absolutely nothing whatever while here, that would not have wanted you to watch me do. There are no temptations for me in Salt Lake, none whatever. Their saloons [might] just as well be in New York, and their girls in Greenland" (Vardis Fisher Collection, Box 1, Folder 2, MSS 5, Arthur Porter Special Collections, Brigham Young University, Idaho). In his next letter, dated October 15, he says, "Honestly, I can't find time to go to church. I did not even get to go to Conference."

16. Woodward, *Tiger*, 75–76.

17. Fisher publications from *The University Pen*. Joseph M. Flora Papers, Box 3, Folder 4, Boise State University Special Collection and Archives, MSS 285. The one-act play, *Dream Shadows* was published in 1923, after Fisher had already moved to Chicago. It was one of five one-act plays that Fisher wrote while studying at the University of Utah. The manuscript copies of all five plays are held in the L. Tom Perry Special Collections Archive at Brigham Young University, MSS 1346.

18. Woodward, *Tiger*, 82.

19. Vardis Fisher letter to "Everybody," December 24, 1921. Fisher Family Papers, Box 1, Folder 10, Boise State University Special Collections and Archives, MSS 160.

20. Qtd. in Woodward, *Tiger*, 85–86.

21. Joseph M. Flora. *Vardis Fisher*. New York: Twayne Publishers, 1965, 20.

22. Wayne Chatterton. *Vardis Fisher: The Frontier and Regional Works*. Boise, ID: Boise State College, 1972, 9.

23. "Sonnets to an Imaginary Madonna: I-X," *Voices; an Open Forum for the*

Poets VI (December 1926/January 1927): 50–55. Vinal edited two publications dedicated to poetry: *Voices: A Journal of Verse*, a bimonthly journal that he began editing in 1921, and the spin-off publication *Voices: An Open Forum for the Poets*, also started in 1921, which published annually.

24. *Vardis Fisher: A Critical Summary, with Notes on His Life and Personality*. Caldwell, ID: Caxton Printers, 1939, 6.

25. For a book-length analysis of all of Fisher's poetry, see Dorys C. Grover's *Vardis Fisher: The Novelist as Poet*. New York: Revisionist Press, 1973.

26. *Vardis Fisher: A Critical Summary*, 6.

27. Themis Chronopoulos. "Urban Decline and the Withdrawal of New York University from University Heights, The Bronx," *Bronx County Historical Society Journal* XLVI, 4–24, 7.

28. *The Little Review* published a portion of the "Nausicaa" chapter of *Ulysses*, and its editors were charged with, and convicted of, violating New York's obscenity laws. This created a de facto ban on *Ulysses* and similar works until 1933, when U.S. District Court judge John M. Woolsey ruled in *United States v. One Book Called Ulysses* that the book was "serious and sincere" literature and not obscene. See Marisa Pagnattaro, "Carving a Literary Exception: The Obscenity Standard and Ulysses." *Twentieth Century Literature* 47.2 (2001): 217–40.

29. Vardis Fisher. *The Caxton Printers in Idaho: A Short History*. Cincinnati: Society of Bibliosophers, 1944, 21.

30. *Vardis Fisher: A Critical Summary*, 7.

31. Fisher, "Comments on His *Testament of Man* Series," 64–65.

32. Milton, et al., *Three West*, 8.

33. Fisher, *The Caxton Printers in Idaho*, in *Thomas Wolfe*, 21.

34. J. H. Gipson. "Publishing in the West" (part 3 of 4). *Ogden Standard-Examiner*, January 8, 1939, 25.

35. Paul E. Johnston. "Caxton Printers, Ltd., Regional Publishers." *Pacific Northwest Quarterly* 48, no. 3 (1957): 100–105.

36. Jerre G. Mangione. *The Dream and the Deal: The Federal Writers' Project, 1935–1943*. Syracuse, NY: Syracuse University Press, 1996, 9.

37. The original offer was for $2,600 a year but was lowered to $2,200 a year with a subsequent telegram. See Mangione, *Dream and the Deal*, 78.

38. Vardis Fisher to Elizabeth Nowell, October 10, 1935. Vardis Fisher Papers. Yale Collection of American Literature, Beinecke Rare Book and Manuscript Library, MSS 555, Box 25. Fisher wrote "PWA" instead of "WPA," or Works Progress Administration, which was the Depression-Era federal agency that oversaw the Federal Writers' Project.

39. Vardis Fisher. "Writers on Relief." *Idaho Statesman*, June 2, 1941, 7.

40. Mangione, *Dream and the Deal*, 201.

41. For a collection of comments from reviewers, see Ronald W. Taber, "Vardis Fisher and the 'Idaho Guide': Preserving Culture for the New Deal." *Pacific Northwest Quarterly* 59, no. 2 (1968): 68–76.

42. Qtd. in Mangione, *Dream and the Deal*, 207.

43. Ibid., 207–28.

44. Alessandro Meregaglia and Laura W. Johnston, eds. *Vardis Fisher's Boise*. Boise Rediscovered Publishing, 2019.

45. Vardis Fisher to Fred Marsh, August 2, 1951. Vardis Fisher Papers. Yale Collection of American Literature, Beinecke Rare Book and Manuscript Library, MSS 555, Box 26.

46. Vardis Fisher to Alfred Knopf, May 31, 1938. Vardis Fisher Papers. Yale Collection of American Literature, Beinecke Rare Book and Manuscript Library, MSS 555, Box 25.

47. James V. D'Arc. "Darrryl F. Zanuck's 'Brigham Young': A Film in Context." *Brigham Young University Studies* 29, no. 1 (Winter 1989): 5–33.

48. "Vardis Fisher Is Taking to the Hills; Quitting Boise to Write Another Novel." *Idaho Statesman*, November 7, 1939, 1.

49. Woodward, *Tiger*, 143–46.

50. Fisher, "The Novelist and His Work," in *Thomas Wolfe*, 108–9.

51. Fisher's account book, which includes information on his income and expenses from 1939 through 1965 (though not always complete information), is now part of the Vardis Fisher Papers at Boise State University (MSS 159, Box 6).

52. Vardis Fisher to Fred Marsh, August 2, 1951. Vardis Fisher Papers. Yale Collection of American Literature, Beinecke Rare Book and Manuscript Library, MSS 555, Box 26.

53. Though his estate would experience similar commercial success posthumously in 1972, when famed director Sidney Pollack acquired the rights to Fisher's 1965 novel, *Mountain Man*, and used it as the basis for the film by the same name starring Robert Redford.

54. Vardis Fisher to Elizabeth Nowell, n.d. Yale Collection of American Literature, Beinecke Rare Book and Manuscript Library, MSS 555, Box 25.

55. Vardis Fisher to Elizabeth Nowell, November 20, 1940.

56. John W. Tebbel. *Between Covers: The Rise and Transformation of Book Publishing in America*. New York: Oxford University Press, 1987, 268–69.

57. Vardis Fisher to James Henle, Vanguard Press, July 7, 1942. Yale Collection of American Literature, Beinecke Rare Book and Manuscript Library, MSS 555, Box 22.

58. Milton, et al., *Three* West, 14.

59. Muriel Fuller to Vardis Fisher, October 2, 1952. Yale Collection of American Literature, Beinecke Rare Book and Manuscript Library, MSS 555, Box 26.

60. Vardis Fisher to James Henle, April 26, 1946. Yale Collection of American Literature, Beinecke Rare Book and Manuscript Library, MSS 555, Box 22.

61. Vardis Fisher to Lynn Garrick, December 15, 1952. Yale Collection of American Literature, Beinecke Rare Book and Manuscript Library, MSS 555, Box 25.

62. Vardis Fisher to Elizabeth Nowell, December 30, 1952. Yale Collection of American Literature, Beinecke Rare Book and Manuscript Library, MSS 555, Box 25.

63. Vardis Fisher to J. H. Gipson. Yale Collection of American Literature, Beinecke Rare Book and Manuscript Library, MSS 555, Box 24.

64. Vardis Fisher to Elizabeth Nowell, January 14, 1955. Yale Collection of American Literature, Beinecke Rare Book and Manuscript Library, MSS 555, Box 25.

65. W. Nelson, and Marilyn Auer. *The Imprint of Alan Swallow: Quality Publishing in the West.* Syracuse, NY: Syracuse University Press, 2014, 101.

66. Alan Swallow. 1915–1966. *An Editor's Essays of Two Decades.* Seattle: Experiment Press; distributed to the trade by A. Swallow, Denver, 1962, 345.

67. Nelson and Auer, *Imprint of Alan Swallow*, 127.

68. Ibid., 95.

69. The cover blurbs are from the Pyramid editions of, respectively, *Darkness and the Deep* (1960), *The Divine Passion* (1961), and *The Golden Rooms* (1962).

70. Vardis Fisher Account Book. Vardis Fisher Papers at Boise State University (MSS 159, Box 6), 210.

71. "Vardis Fisher Feted." *Idaho Free Press*, January 31, 1968, 12.

72. "Vardis Fisher Dies from Pills." *South Idaho Press*, July 12, 1968, 1.

73. Tim Woodward. "Papers Donated to BSU Paint More Complete Picture of Author." *Idaho Statesman*, June 15, 1997, 46.

74. Opal Laurel Holmes, "Vardis Fisher Was Not a Mormon," press release, Vardis Fisher Collection, Boise State University, n.d. (ca. 1979). Holmes included this press release, and the corresponding open letter to Spencer W. Kimball, as appendix to all of Fisher's works for which she held the copyrights and was able to republish under her own imprint.

75. Stephen L. Tanner. "Vardis Fisher and the Mormons," in *Rediscovering Vardis Fisher: Centennial Essays*, ed. Joseph M. Flora. Moscow: University of Idaho Press, 2000), 100–101.

76. Irene Fisher Mead to Leonard Arrington, June 15, 1976; qtd. in Arrington and Haupt, "Mormon Heritage," 30.

77. Mick McAllister. "Vardis Fisher's Mormon Heritage Re-Examined: A Critical Response." At Wanderer's Well. http://www.dancingbadger.com/vf-mormonf.htm (November, 2001).

78. Vardis Fisher. *We Are Betrayed.* Caldwell, ID: Caxton Printers, 1935, 33–34.

79. Milton, et al., *Three West*, 3–4. Two years after Fisher's death, Milton published this interview in his book *Three West*, which was almost immediately assailed by Opal Laurel Holmes as a betrayal of her late husband's legacy. She wrote letters to Milton and to the president of the University of South Dakota demanding that the book be recalled and threatening to sue if it was not. See Joseph M. Flora, "Remembering Vardis and Opal Fisher" in *Idaho Yesterdays* 50, no. 2 (Fall 2009): 20. Retrieved November 28, 2013, from http://134.50.3.223/idahoyesterdays/index.php/IY/article/view/16/13.

80. Joseph M. Flora. "Vardis Fisher and the Mormons." *Dialogue: A Journal of Mormon Thought* 4, no. 3 (Autumn 1969): 48.

Chapter Two. Vardis Fisher and the Beginnings of Mormon Regionalism

1. Faulkner's *Sartoris*, the first Yoknapatawpha novel, was published in January 1929. Steinbeck's *Cup of Gold*, Caldwell's *The Bastard*, and Wolfe's *Look Homeward, Angel* were all also published in 1929.

2. See John Peale Bishop, "The Strange Case of Vardis Fisher" in *Southern Review* (Autumn 1937): 348–59; George Dixon Snell, "Erskine Caldwell and Vardis Fisher: The Nearly Animal Kingdom," in *Shapers of American Fiction 1798–1847.* New York: Dutton, 1947, 263–88.

3. Ray B. West. *Writing in the Rocky Mountains.* Lincoln: University of Nebraska Press, 1947, 18.

4. D. W. Meinig. "The Mormon Culture Region: Strategies and Patterns in the Geography of the American West, 1847–1964." *Annals of the Association of American Geographers* 55, no. 2 (June 1965): 191, 195, 220.

5. Ethan R. Yorgason. *Transformation of the Mormon Culture Region.* Urbana: University of Illinois Press, 2003, 19.

6. For a complete bibliography along with four representative examples, see Michael Austin and Ardis Parshall, eds., *Dime Novel Mormons*, Draper, UT: Greg Kofford Books, 2017.

7. The term *Home Literature* was first introduced by LDS Apostle Orson F. Whitney in an essay with that title in the July 1988 issue of *The Contributor*. Whitney himself was an important author of Mormon Home Literature, with his 1904 long poem *Elias*. Other noted authors included B. H. Roberts (also a Mormon general authority), Nephi Anderson, Josephine Spencer, and Brigham Young's daughter, Susa Gates Young.

8. All were published jointly by Caxton Printers of Caldwell, Idaho, and Doubleday, Doran & Co. of New York, with Caxton serving as the first edition of record.

9. Vardis Fisher. *Toilers of the Hills*. Boston: Houghton Mifflin, 1928; *Dark Bridwell*, Boston: Houghton Mifflin, 1931; *April*, New York: Doubleday, Doran & Company, 1937.

10. "Antelope People: 'Slim Scott,' 'Susan Hemp,' 'Konrad Myrdton,'" *Voices: An Open Forum for the Poets* VII (March 1928): 203–4; "Antelope People: The North Family—'Charles North,' 'Baby North,' 'Lizzy North,' 'Sally North,' 'Jess North,'" *Voices: A Journal of Verse*, no. 49 (April 1929): 134–36; "'Slim Scott,' 'Susan Hemp,' 'Konrad Myrdton,' 'Perg Jasper,' 'Joe Hunter,'" [Poems] in Northwest Verse; an Anthology, ed., Harold G. Merriam. Caldwell, ID: Caxton Printers, 1931, 139.

11. Fisher, *April*, 53.

12. Ibid., 50, 59.

13. Vardis Fisher. "Antelope People: The North Family—'Charles North,' 'Baby North,' 'Lizzy North,' 'Sally North,' 'Jess North.'" *Voices: A Journal of Verse*, no. 49 (April 1929): 134–36.

14. Dale Morgan's *Mormon Storytellers* first appeared in the Fall 1942 issue of *Rocky Mountain Review*. Cited from Eugene England and Lavina Fielding Anderson, eds., *Tending the Garden*, Salt Lake City: Signature Books, 1996, 8.

15. Milton, et al., *Three West*, 3.

16. John Peale Bishop. "The Strange Case of Vardis Fisher," Edmund Wilson, ed., *Collected Essays of John Peale Bishop*. New York: Octagon, 1975, 58.

17. From their earliest days in the Salt Lake Valley, the Latter-day Saint pioneers took the prophecy in Isaiah 35:1—that "the desert shall rejoice, and blossom as the rose" as a description of their own work turning the Great Basin Desert into a flourishing homeland.

18. "Joe Hunter." *Northwest Verse: An Anthology*, ed., Harold G. Merriam. Caldwell, ID: Caxton Printers, 1931.

19. *Vardis Fisher: A Critical Summary, with Notes on His Life and Personality*. Caldwell, ID: Caxton Printers, 1939, 6.

20. Fisher, *Toilers of the Hills*, 200.

21. Ibid., 339.

22. Fisher, *Dark Bridwell*, 19–20.

23. Ibid., 22.

24. Vardis Fisher. "The Novelist and His Work," in *Thomas Wolfe as I Knew Him and Other Essays*. Denver: Alan Swallow, 1963, 109.

25. In *Tiger on the Road*, Tim Woodward quotes Fisher's third wife, Opal Holmes, as saying, "Vardis gave a bit of thought to death, and he was a man

who could get very unhappy and morose. It was possible, in the months after Leona's death, that he came very close" (98–99).

26. Vardis Fisher. "A Trivial Excursion in Modesty." *Antioch Review* 2, no. 1 (1942): 126.

27. Vardis Fisher. *In Tragic Life*. Caldwell, ID: Caxton Printers, 1932, 32.

28. Ibid., 102–3.

29. Ibid., 151–52, 154.

30. Ibid., 173.

31. Ibid., 449.

32. Vardis Fisher. *We Are Betrayed*. Garden City, NY: Doubleday, Doran & Co., 1935, 253.

33. Fisher, *In Tragic Life*, 23, 30.

34. Ibid., 363–64.

35. Ibid., 362.

36. Ibid., 383.e.

37. Ibid., 446.

38. Ibid., 448.

39. Ibid., 449.

40. Ibid., 460–61, 462, 464.

Chapter Three. *Children of God* and the Golden Age of Mormon Literature

1. Bernard DeVoto. "Fossil Remnants of the Frontier: Notes on a Utah Boyhood," in *Forays and Rebuttals*. New York: Little, Brown, 1936, 31. See also Leland Fetzer, "Bernard DeVoto and the Mormon Tradition" in *Dialogue: A Journal of Mormon Thought* 7, no. 3–4 (Autumn/Winter 1973): 23–37.

2. Bernard DeVoto. "Vacation." *Harper's*, October 1938, 560.

3. Vardis Fisher to Elizabeth Nowell, July 9, 1938. Yale Collection of American Literature, Beinecke Rare Book and Manuscript Library, MSS 555, Box 25.

4. Vardis Fisher. *God or Caesar? The Writing of Fiction for Beginners*. Caldwell, ID: Caxton Printers, 1953, 241–42.

5. Vardis Fisher to Alfred Knopf, May 31, 1938. Yale Collection of American Literature, Beinecke Rare Book and Manuscript Library, MSS 555, Box 25.

6. Vardis Fisher to Elizabeth Nowell, October 21, 1938. Yale Collection of American Literature, Beinecke Rare Book and Manuscript Library, MSS 555, Box 25.

7. Vardis Fisher to Elizabeth Nowell, September 8, 1938. Yale Collection of American Literature, Beinecke Rare Book and Manuscript Library, MSS 555, Box 25.

8. Vardis Fisher to Elizabeth Nowell, September 13, 1938. Yale Collection of American Literature, Beinecke Rare Book and Manuscript Library, MSS 555, Box 25.

9. "Mormon Empire History Theme of Fisher Story Winning $7,500 Contest." *Idaho Statesman*, June 27, 1939, 12.

10. In a review of *Children of God*, DeVoto revisits his statement that "there would never be a good novel about the Mormons" and concludes "that, like Joseph's date for the end of the world, was bad prophecy." "Millennial Millions," *Saturday Review of Literature*, August 26, 1939, 4.

11. Joseph Smith—*History* 1: 8–20.

12. Vardis Fisher. *Children of God*. New York: Harper, 1939, 5.

13. Vardis Fisher. *In Tragic Life*. Caldwell, ID: Caxton Printers, 1932, 152–55.

14. Fisher, *Children of God*, 18.

15. Ibid., 127.

16. Ibid., 89.

17. Ibid., 168.

18. Ibid., 187.

19. Ibid., 244.

20. Elder John A. Widtsoe, an influential LDS Apostle in the mid-20th century, wrote in his book *Evidences and Reconciliations*: "The United States census records from 1850 to 1940, and all available Church records, uniformly show a preponderance of males in Utah and in the Church. Indeed, the excess in Utah has usually been larger than for the whole United States, as would be expected in a pioneer state. The births within the Church obey the usual population law—a slight excess of males. Orson Pratt, writing in 1853 from direct knowledge of Utah conditions, when the excess of females was supposedly the highest, declares against the opinion that females outnumbered the males in Utah. The theory that plural marriage was a consequence of a surplus of female Church members fails from lack of evidence." John A. Widtsoe. *Evidences and Reconciliations*. Salt Lake City: Bookcraft, 1943, 391.

21. *Brigham's Destroying Angel, Being the Life, Confession, and Startling Disclosures of the Notorious Bill Hickman, the Danite Chief of Utah*, ed., J. H. Beadle. New York: Crofutt, 1872.

22. Davis Bitton. "Mormon Biography." *Biography* 4, no.1 (Winter 1981): 9.

23. Fisher, *Children of God*, 427.

24. For Fisher's own political leanings, see "Some Implications of Radicalism," in *The Neurotic Nightingale* (Milwaukee, WI: Casanova Press, 1935), 40–58; and "Communism and Emperor Worship," in *Thomas Wolfe as I Knew Him and Other Essays* (Denver: Alan Swallow, 1963), 128–41.

25. Fisher, *Children of God*, 587–88.

26. Somewhat implausibly, Moroni McBride is an adult convert to Mormonism, despite sharing his name with one of the key figures of the Book of Mormon.

27. Fisher, *Children of God*, 619.

28. Ibid., 763.

29. Ibid., 764.

30. Vardis Fisher. "The Mormons." *Transatlantic*, no. 9 (May 1944): 43.

31. Matthew Bowman. *The Mormon People*. New York: Random House, 2014, 178–79.

32. Joseph M. Flora. *Vardis Fisher*. New York: Twayne, 1965, 132.

33. Tim Woodward. *Tiger on the Road: The Life of Vardis Fisher*. Caldwell, ID: Caxton Printers, 1989, 149.

34. "*Children of God* by Vardis Fisher Is Not a Historical Novel." The Vardis Fisher Collection. WSU Stewart Library Special Collections, MSS-2, Folder 3. First published in *The Richmond Missourian*, April 29, 1940.

35. The only copy of the review that I have been able to locate is in the Kenneth Macgowan Collection at UCLA attached to a letter that Widtsoe wrote to Macgowan dated September 8, 1939. Papers, Box 28, Folder 8.

36. John A. Widtsoe to Kenneth Macgowan, September 7, 1939. Kenneth Macgowan Papers (Collection 887). Department of Special Collections, Charles E. Young Research Library, University of California, Los Angeles, Box 28, Folder 8.

37. John A. Widtsoe to Mrs. George L. Zundell, January 12, 1940. John Widtsoe Papers CR 712/2, Box 173, Folder 13.

38. James V. D'Arc. "Darryl F. Zanuck's *Brigham Young*: A Film in Context." *BYU Studies* 29, no. 1 (Winter 1989): 9–10.

39. Vardis Fisher to Elizabeth Nowell, June 5, 1939, and September 25, 1840. Yale Collection of American Literature, Beinecke Rare Book and Manuscript Library, MSS 555, Box 25.

40. John A. Widtsoe to Kenneth Macgowan, September 7, 1939. Kenneth Macgowan Papers (Collection 887). Department of Special Collections, Charles E. Young Research Library, University of California, Los Angeles, Box 28, Folder 8.

41. Kenneth Macgowan to Heber J. Grant, Augusts 29, 1939. Kenneth Macgowan Papers (Collection 887). Department of Special Collections, Charles E. Young Research Library, University of California, Los Angeles, Box 28, Folder 8.

42. D'Arc, "Zanuck's *Brigham Young*," 11.

43. Kenneth Macgowan to Harry Brand, April 30, 1940. Kenneth Macgowan Papers, Box 28, Folder 8.

44. Paul Bailey, *For This My Glory* (Los Angeles: Lyman House, 1940); Jean Woodman, *Glory Spent* (New York: Carrick & Evans, 1940); Rhoda Nelson, *This Is Freedom* (New York: Dodd & Mead, 1941); Maurine Whipple, *The Giant Joshua* (Boston: Houghton Mifflin, 1941); Lorene Pearson, *Harvest Waits* (Indianapolis: Bobbs-Merrill, 1941); Hoffman Birney, *Ann Carmeny* (New York: G. P. Putnam's Sons, 1941); Virginia Sorensen, *A Little Lower than the Angels* (New York: Knopf, 1942); Elinore Pryor, *And Never Yield* (New York: Macmillan, 1942).

45. Between 1895 and 1940, Deseret News Press published some two dozen works of faith-promoting fiction aimed at LDS audiences. Among the most popular were Nephi Anderson's *Added Upon* (1898), Susa Young Gates's *John Stevens' Courtship* (1911), and Alfred Osmond's *Married Sweethearts: A Romance of the Rockies* (1928).

46. Transcript of recorded interview of Jean Maw Woodman by Dennis Rowley, June 10, 1989. Jean Maw Woodman Papers, MSS 1791. L. Tom Perry Special Collections, Harold B. Lee Library, Brigham Young University, Box 1, Folder 1.

47. Lynn Carrick to Jean Woodman, August 11, 139. Jean Maw Woodman Papers, MSS 1791. L. Tom Perry Special Collections, Harold B. Lee Library, Brigham Young University, Box 1, Folder 5.

48. Marian Howe Broaddus. Review of *Glory Spent* by Jean Woodman, *El Paso Times* (El Paso, Texas), June 9, 1940, 6.

49. Stephen Vincent Benet. "Pioneering: Utah to New York City," *New York Herald Tribune*, April 29, 1940, qtd. in "'Glory Spent,' Woodman Novel Reviewed by New York Critics," *Daily Herald*, Provo, UT, May 20, 1940, 4.

50. Phyllis McGinley to Lynn Carrick, Jean Maw Woodman Papers, Box 1, Folder 5.

51. Frank C. Robertson. "Former Provo Woman Writes Novel with Utah Background," *Daily Herald*, Provo, UT, April 24, 1940, 10.

52. Vardis Fisher. "Bleak Emotional Bondage: *Glory Spent, by Jean Woodman,*" *Saturday Review*, May 25, 1940, 14.

53. Paul Bailey to Charles Palmer, March 19, 1940. Paul Dayton Bailey Papers, Utah State Historical Society, MSS B414, Box 17, Folder 1941.

54. For an article-length analysis of the correspondence between Widtsoe and Bailey on this and other books, see Michael Austin and Ardis Parshall, "The Novelist and the Apostle: Paul Bailey, John A. Widtsoe, and the Quest for Faithful Fiction in the 1940s." *Journal of Mormon History* 42, no.3 (July 2016): 183–210.

55. Paul Bailey to Sydney A. Sanders, December 7, 1941. Paul Dayton Bailey Papers, Utah State Historical Society, MSS B414, Box 17, Folder 1941.

56. Veda Tebbs Hale. *Swell Suffering: A Biography of Maurine Whipple*. Salt Lake City: Greg Kofford, 2011, 133.

57. Maurine Whipple. *The Giant Joshua*. New York: Houghton Mifflin, 1941, 620.

58. The noted Mormon critic Eugene England, for example, called the giant "Whipple's The Giant Joshua: The Greatest but Not the Great Mormon Novel," in *Association for Mormon Letters Annual*, 2001, 61. Terryl L. Givens refers to *People of Paradox: A History of Mormon Culture* (New York: Oxford University Press, 2007) 291.

59. Sorensen, *A Little Lower than the Angels*, 113–15.

60. Wallace Stegner. Review of *A Little Lower than the Angels*, *Saturday Review*, May 9, 1942, 11.

61. Alfred Knopf to Virginia Sorensen, January 7, 1942, qtd. in Mary Bradford and Virginia Sorensen, *A Little Lower than the Angels*. Salt Lake City: Signature Books, 1997, ix.

62. Dale L. Morgan. "Mormon Storytellers." *Rocky Mountain Review* 7 (Fall 1942): 1, 3–7. Reprinted in Eugene England and Lavina F. Anderson. *Tending the Garden: Essays on Mormon Literature*. Salt Lake City: Signature Books, 1996, 3. Morgan counts *Children of God* itself as one of the nine and includes the eight novels listed in Note 44 previously.

63. Jonreed Lauritzen, *Arrows into the Sun* (New York: Knopf, 1943); Paul Bailey, *The Gay Saint* (Hollywood: Murray & Gee, 1944); Richard Scowcroft, *Children of the Covenant* (Boston: Houghton Mifflin, 1946); Virginia Sorensen, *On This Star* (New York: Reynal & Hitchcock, 1946); Paul Bailey, *Song Everlasting* (Los Angeles: Westernlore, 1946); Helen Hinckley, *The Mountains Are Mine* (New York: Vanguard, 1948); Blanche Cannon, *Nothing Ever Happens Sunday Morning* (New York: Putnam, 1948); Samuel Taylor, *Heaven Knows Why* (New York: A. A. Wyn, 1948); Paul Bailey, *Jacob Hamblin: Buckskin Apostle* (Los Angeles: Westernlore, 1948); Jonreed Lauritzen, *Song before Sunrise* (New York: Doubleday, 1948); Virginia Sorensen, *The Evening and the Morning* (New York: Harcourt, 1949); Ardyth Kennelly, *The Peaceable Kingdom* (Boston: Houghton Mifflin, 1949).

64. Kennelly's hometown newspaper reported in 1950 that *Peaceable Kingdom* had sold 450,000 copies in its first year. *Albany Democrat-Herald*, September 10, 1955, 7.

65. The term "Lost Generation" appears to have been introduced into Mormon literary study by BYU Professor Edward Geary who, in the second meeting of the Association for Mormon Letters in 1977, presented a paper entitled

"Mormondom's Lost Generation: The Novelists of the 1940s"—a paper, that has since been reprinted several times and has become a standard starting point for the construction of a Mormon literary canon.

Chapter Four. The Not Quite Not Mormon
Worldview of the *Testament of Man*

1. Tim Woodward. *Tiger on the Road*. Caldwell, ID: Caxton Printers, 1989, 160.

2. The Revisionist Press of New York, an academic press that specialized in unrevised dissertations, published a series on Vardis Fisher in the 1970s. Among the titles it produced entirely or partially about *The Testament of Man* are: Alfred K. Thomas' *The Epic of Evolution, Its Etiology and Art: A Study of Vardis Fisher's Testament of Man* (1973); Doris C. Grover's *A Solitary Voice: Vardis Fisher* (1973); George F. Day's *The Uses of History in the Novels of Vardis Fisher* (1976); and *The Past in the Present: Two Essays on History and Myth in Vardis Fisher's Testament of Man* (1979). In addition to these titles, Joseph M. Flora's dissertation at the University of Michigan in 1962, "Vardis Fisher's Story of Vridar Hunter: A Study in Theory and Revision," deals at least partially with *The Testament*.

3. Marilyn Trent Grunkmeyer, "An Anthropological View of the *Testament of Man*," in Joseph M. Flora, ed., *Rediscovering Vardis Fisher*. Moscow: University of Idaho Press, 2000, 165–66. The "perduring male fantasy" that Grunkmeyer refers to is "a fantasy that the past was a universal matriarchy that was overcome by universal patriarchy." This transition from matriarchy to patriarchy is indeed an important part of the series, and especially of its third, fourth, and fifth books. However, it is at least arguable that Fisher did not intend to portray either the matriarchy or the patriarchy as "universal"—but to represent, instead, the specific development of the group of people who ended up becoming the Hebrews.

4. Fisher explains his research for the *Testament* in some detail in the essay "Comments on His *Testament of Man Series*" in his book of occasional writings, *Thomas Wolfe as I Knew Him and Other Essays*. Denver: Alan Swallow, 1963, 64–78.

5. Since 1982, all editions of the Book of Mormon published by the Church of Jesus Christ of Latter-day Saints have carried the subtitle "Another Testament of Jesus Christ."

6. For the Book of Mormon's use of these types, see Michael Austin, "How the Book of Mormon Reads the Bible: A Theory of Types." *Journal of Book of Mormon Studies* 26 (2017): 48–81.

7. Vardis Fisher. *Darkness and the Deep*. New York: Vanguard, 1943, 17.

8. Marilyn Trent Grunkmeyer. "An Anthropological View of the *Testament of Man*," in Flora, ed., *Rediscovering Vardis Fisher*, 167–68.

9. The hypothesis that the Neanderthals' extinction was the result of conflict with the Cro-Magnon—the ancestors of modern *homo sapiens*—was first introduced in 1912 by French paleontologist Marcellin Boule. Near the end of the second volume in the series, *The Golden Rooms* (New York: Pyramid, 1962), Fisher announces his support for this hypothesis by having a Cro-Magnon character murder his Neanderthal counterpart and then generalizing to a larger massacre: "Gode and his companions had been driven to murder because of outraged self-love. Other men would go on killing the bent-legged and stoop-shouldered dwarves until they had exterminated practically all of Harg's people" (293).

10. Cynthia Eller has chronicled and thoroughly debunked the 19th-century hypothesis of prehistoric matriarchal societies in two book-length studies: *The Myth of Matriarchal Prehistory: Why an Invented Past Won't Give Women a Future* (Boston: Beacon Press, 2006) and *Gentlemen and Amazons: The Myth of Matriarchal Prehistory, 1861–1900* (Berkeley: University of California Press, 2011). The idea was not common when Fisher wrote *Intimations of Eve* and *Adam and the Serpent*, but it still had proponents in the early 20th century, when some of the books that Fisher relied on were written. In his interview with Swallow, Fisher credited the idea to an "almost casual remark" by the eminent Yale sociologist William Graham Sumner, who said "It may well be believed that the change from the mother family to the father family is the greatest and most revolutionary in the history of civilization" (Swallow, *Thomas Wolfe as I Knew Him*, 25). Sumner did indeed make this argument in 1909. William G. Sumner, "The Family and Social Change." *American Journal of Sociology* XIV, no. 5 (March 1909): 581–82.

11. Vardis Fisher. *The Divine Passion* (New York: Vanguard, 1948). For various Exodus-inspired tropes, see: "milk and honey," p. 291; "burning bush," p. 156; atonement sacrifices, pp. 224–26; "covenant," p. 216; The Ten Commandments, pp. 112–16.; and "chosen people," p. 292.

12. Vardis Fisher. *Intimations of Eve*. New York: Vantage, 1946, 173–74.

13. Vardis Fisher. *Adam and the Serpent*. New York: Vantage, 1947, 209–10.

14. Vardis Fisher. *Orphans in Gethsemane*. Denver: Alan Swallow, 1960, 52.

15. Fisher, "Comments," 75.

16. In the fourth chapter of *Culture and Anarchy*, Matthew Arnold describes "Hebraism and Hellenism" as two universal dispositions that reached a sort of perfection in the cultures for which they are named. "The uppermost idea

with Hellenism is to see things as they really are; the uppermost idea with Hebraism is conduct and obedience." Matthew Arnold, *Culture and Anarchy*, ed., Jane Garnett, Oxford, UK: Oxford University Press, 2006, 97.

17. Fisher does not use the term *Hasidim* to describe the conservative Jews in *The Island of the Innocent*. The term, though, is often used in discussions of the period, including Alfred K. Thomas' 1973 study of *Testament of Man*.

18. Vardis Fisher. *Island of the Innocent*. New York: Abelard, 1952, 1.

19. Ibid., 96.

20. Ibid., 238.

21. Ibid., 264.

22. Ibid., 266.

23. Vardis Fisher. *A Goat for Azazel*. Denver: Alan Swallow, 22–23.

24. Ibid., 24.

25. The text dates Damon's death by placing it "in the Fifteenth Year of Trajan's reign," or approximately 113 (Fisher, *Azazel*, 295).

26. See Leviticus 16:8–10.

27. Fisher, *Azazel*, 294.

28. Ibid., 299.

29. Ibid., 303.

30. Virginia Sorensen's Mormon-themed books include the novels *A Little Lower than the Angels* (Knopf, 1942), *On This Star* (Reynal & Hitchcock, 1946), *The Evening and the Morning* (Harcourt & Brace, 1949), *Many Heavens* (Harcourt & Brace, 1954), and *Kingdom Come* (Harcourt & Brace, 1960). Mormonism also features prominently in her memoir, *Where Nothing Is Long Ago* (Harcourt & Brace, 1963).

31. Juanita Brooks's *Mountain Meadows Massacre* (Norman: University of Oklahoma Press, 1950) was the first book-length study of one of the most controversial events in Mormon history; Maurine Whipple's *The Giant Joshua* (Houghton Mifflin, 1942), which deals with polygamy, the colonization of Southern Utah, and (tangentially) the Mountain Meadows Massacre remains one of the most important Mormon novels ever written.

32. Samuel Taylor (1907–1997) was the grandson of John Taylor, the third president of the LDS Church and the son of John W. Taylor, an apostle who was excommunicated in 1911 for continuing to practice polygamy after the Manifesto forbidding it. His historical works include *Nightfall at Nauvoo* (1971), a historical novel; *The Kingdom or Nothing* (1976), a biography of his grandfather; and *Family Kingdom* (1951), a biography of his father.

33. Vardis Fisher. *We Are Betrayed* (Caldwell, ID: Caxton Printers, 1935), 219.

34. Ibid.

A Bibliographic Essay

1. "Antelope People: 'Slim Scott,' 'Susan Hemp,' 'Konrad Myrdton.'" *Voices; an Open Forum for the Poets* VII (March 1928): 203–4; "Antelope People: The North Family—'Charles North,' 'Baby North,' 'Lizzy North,' 'Sally North,' 'Jess North.'" *Voices: A Journal of Verse* no. 49 (April 1929): 134–36; "'Slim Scott,' 'Susan Hemp,' 'Konrad Myrdton,' 'Perg Jasper,' 'Joe Hunter,'" [Poems] in Northwest Verse; an Anthology, ed., Harold G. Merriam. Caldwell, ID: Caxton Printers, 1931.

2. Vardis Fisher. "Hometown Revisited," in *Thomas Wolfe as I Knew Him and Other Essays*. Denver: Alan Swallow, 1963, 116–17.

3. Edward Geary. "Women Regionalists of Mormon Country" in Emily Toth, *Regionalism and the Female Imagination: A Collection of Essays* (New York: Human Sciences Press, 1985, 139–52, 2); "The Poetics of Provincialism: Mormon Regional Fiction," *Dialogue* 11, no. 2 (Summer 1978): 3, 15–243; "Mormondom's Lost Generation: The Novelists of the 1940s" *BYU Studies Quarterly* 18, no. 1 (Spring 1978).

4. James E. Starrs and Kira Gale, *The Death of Meriwether Lewis: A Historic Crime Scene Investigation* (Chicago: River Junction Press, 2012), 58–59; Adam M. Sowards, *Idaho's Place: A New History of the Gem State* (Seattle: University of Washington Press, 2016), 238–43; Elisa Leonelli, *Robert Redford and the American West: A Critical Essay* (Philadelphia: Xlibris, 2007), 42–54.

Index

MICHAEL AUSTIN is the executive vice president for academic affairs at the University of Evansville, and he was previously a professor of English. His many books include *Rereading Job: Understanding the Ancient World's Greatest Poem* and *We Must Not Be Enemies: Restoring America's Civic Tradition*.

Introductions to Mormon Thought

The University of Illinois Press
is a founding member of the
Association of University Presses.

———————————————

Composed in 10.75/14 Adobe Minion Pro
with DIN display
by Jim Proefrock
at the University of Illinois Press
Manufactured by Sheridan Books, Inc.

University of Illinois Press
1325 South Oak Street
Champaign, IL 61820-6903
www.press.uillinois.edu